THE Micro-Brewery HANDBOOK

DC REEVES

CRAFT, BREW, & BUILD YOUR OWN
MICROBREWERY SUCCESS

WILEY

Published by John Wiley & Sons, Inc., Hoboken, New Jersey.
Published simultaneously in Canada.

For general information on our other products and services or for technical support, please contact our Customer Care Department within the United States at (800) 762–2974, outside the United States at (317) 572–3993, or fax (317) 572–4002.

Wiley publishes in a variety of print and electronic formats and by print-on-demand. Some material included with standard print versions of this book may not be included in e-books or in print-on-demand. If this book refers to media such as a CD or DVD that is not included in the version you purchased, you may download this material at http://booksupport.wiley.com. For more information about Wiley products, visit www.wiley.com.

Library of Congress Cataloging-in-Publication Data:

Names: Reeves, D. C., author.
Title: The microbrewery handbook : craft, brew, and build your own
   microbrewery success / D.C. Reeves.
Description: Hoboken, New Jersey : John Wiley & Sons, Inc., [2020] |
   Includes index.
Identifiers: LCCN 2019029944 (print) | LCCN 2019029945 (ebook) | ISBN
   9781119598046 (paperback) | ISBN 9781119598039 (adobe pdf) | ISBN
   9781119598053 (epub)
Subjects: LCSH: Microbreweries. | Beer industry. | New business
   enterprises.
Classification: LCC HD9397.A2 R44 2020 (print) | LCC HD9397.A2 (ebook) |
   DDC 663/.42068—dc23
LC record available at https://lccn.loc.gov/2019029944
LC ebook record available at https://lccn.loc.gov/2019029945

COVER DESIGN: PAUL MCCARTHY
COVER ART: GETTY IMAGES | STEWART WALLER

Printed in the United States of America

F10014811_101819

For my wonderful daughter Caroline. No matter where it takes us from here, life's greatest reward will always be you.

Contents

Foreword

THERE ARE THREE important reasons why you would want to read this book:

1. You have a great idea for a craft beer bar, cidery, distillery and/or microbrewery.
2. You have great passion for beer in general and all things beer related.
3. You want a solid lesson about the tricky process of successfully starting a business – any business.

D.C. Reeves is an interesting fellow. He has incredible organizational skills. At age 31, he became chief of staff for a major business player in the Florida economy. At 32, while managing the affairs of his very busy boss, D.C. planned and executed his own business startup, Perfect Plain Brewing Company, one of the most successful young microbreweries in the state of Florida. Perfect Plain stays packed with avid beer aficionados. He balanced the achievement of all his business success with taking care of a delightful young daughter, Caroline.

Clearly, then, D.C. Reeves is organized, he is well rounded, and he thoroughly understands both the microbrewery industry and the business side of corporate success, including both large and small corporations. That makes him a good man to listen to. The fact that D.C. is a former journalist, a sports writer for 10 years, is a bonus. It makes this book a fascinating read.

Enough about D.C.'s credentials; let's talk about the book. This book was written to bridge a gap. On one side we have a superb beer technician with a burning idea about a microbrewery, and on the other side we have the box of knowledge and skills requisite to business success in that industry. This book is transportation over that bridge of challenges.

In my 40 years at Waffle House, America's iconic 24-hour restaurant company, I saw first-hand confirmation of the old saying "Great players don't always make great coaches." In the early years of our growth at Waffle House, we tried fruitlessly to turn great cooks into restaurant managers. We ignored the fact that the skill set involved in being a superb technician does not necessarily translate to the understanding of successful management and leadership principles. This same truth also applies across all industries and to the businesses within each. Just because you can "do" doesn't mean you can lead or manage. You might have a fantastic idea and still fail miserably because, in the end, execution wins out over brilliance, every time.

I wrote a leadership book called *Find an Old Gorilla*. The title is crazy, but the premise is this: if you wake up one morning and realize you have to go through a jungle, it would make sense to find an old gorilla and take him or her along because the old gorillas know where all the good paths are – and also the quicksand.

So, if you are interested in, are considering the pursuit of, or are actually engaged in the craft brewing and/or the microbrewery business, D.C. Reeves is your old gorilla. He has a track record of demonstrated business success, he understands beer and beer production, he speaks fluent leadership and management (including start-up management), and he wrote this book for you.

—**Bert Thornton**
Vice Chairman Emeritus,
Former President and COO,
Waffle House, Inc

Acknowledgments

WITHOUT THE HELP of so many important people, this journey would not have been taken, these lessons would not have been learned, and this book would not exist.

Our Pensacola community, which has embraced us and continues to motivate us to try bigger and better things. Thank you for believing in us and for becoming a hometown that makes us proud.

My parents: my mom, Connie Bookman, and stepfather, Alan Bookman, my father, Jim Reeves, and my stepmother, Susan Reeves, who have been unwavering supporters in my family, my life and my career.

My brother, J.J. Reeves, and my sister-in-law, Lindsay Reeves, for wearing our shirts and being amazing stewards of Perfect Plain, even when you're three states away.

My stepbrother, Jack Johnson, his wife, Kimeran, and their children, Barrett and Irelyn. While sitting in my car parked just two blocks from where Perfect Plain would open, Jack was the first person I talked to in 2015 when I decided I'd make a run at opening my own brewery (even if it just seemed impossible then). Thank you for your friendship, support, and confidence in this crazy idea way back when.

Reed Odeneal, the co-founder and Director of Brewing Operations at Perfect Plain. He was the brains and heart behind our brewing program, and I would not have dared to take this journey without his knowledge, work ethic, and expertise.

Quint and Rishy Studer, whose mentorship, guidance, support, and immense flexibility with my time as his employee has allowed this journey to happen. Perfect Plain would not exist without them.

Shannon Reeves, Caroline's mom, who allowed me to chase dreams all those years.

Our staff at Perfect Plain Brewing Company and Garden & Grain: Bryant Liggett, Nate Simmons, Chrissy Helvenston, Derek Barney, Billy Looney, Sarah Hutchins, Jeff Belot, Jessi Dosen, Jacob Mata, Brad Foster and Nic Gable. I work harder and rest a little easier because of this amazing team. Thank you for your passion, work ethic, and the pride you take in Perfect Plain. I'm proud to say you all work for our company.

Our co-investors, Josh Sitton, Kristen Sitton, and Robert Davis, for believing and trusting in a first-time business owner and a first-time brewing operations manager. We promised we'd bring something new to our community and we hope we've made you proud.

Randall Wells for all of the "pro bono" business and financial advice. We're a fortunate recipient of your passion to help entrepreneurs whenever you can.

Bert Thornton, for all of the kind words and those Sorrento Road Waffle House lunches that brought me so much knowledge and confidence.

Scott Zepp, the co-founder of World of Beer, who was always a helpful ear and whose positive words and outlook gave me the courage to take this entrepreneurial journey.

Dottie DeHart of Dehart and Co. as well as Matthew Holt, Brian Neill, and Peter Knox at John Wiley & Sons for all of your help in making this book possible.

Lisa Nellessen Savage, Jake Newby, Jim Little, Kevin Robinson, and Andy Marlette at the *Pensacola News Journal* and Rick Outzen and Joani Delezen at the *Independent Weekly* in Pensacola for sharing our start and the growth of our company with our Pensacola community. A big thank you to Lisa and Kaycee Lagarde for help with the final editing of this book and saving me from my own procrastination.

Kevin Hagen, our general contractor at H&H Building Group, who has put up with us on two projects and counting. Thank you for always picking up the phone, never freaking out when we change our minds, and for giving us a great example of what a customer-contractor relationship should be like.

Danny Zimmern, who helped us find our perfect building at 50 E. Garden St.

James Hosman, for all of the guidance through our first Small Business Administration loan. I always appreciate you lending your ear.

Our PPBC Founder's Club Members. Thank you for your unwavering support and investing in us before we ever opened. We'll always be grateful for your support.

Beach Community Bank for taking a chance on first-time business owners as well as Hancock/Whitney Bank for believing in our company's vision for the future.

Barbara Scott Payne and Nicole Webb, who have always been helpful when my life as a half employee/half entrepreneur was (and still is) rather crazy.

The leaders at the Studer Family of Companies, who have helped me develop and grow as a business owner. I'd venture to guess some of this book will sound quite familiar.

Gene Williams, the owner of Warchant.com. He hired me as his managing editor in Tallahassee, Florida, and I had a chance to meet and work with our part-time IT/video extraordinaire Reed Odeneal, marking the unofficial start of this craft beer journey.

My great bosses in my previous life, Bill Vilona and Bob Heist of the *Pensacola News Journal* and Tommy Deas of the *Tuscaloosa News*. You taught me many lessons, both in how to be a writer and how to be a reporter, that in some backwards way ended up with me *not* writing football, but beer instead.

Dennis Richards and Mirror Image Brewing Co. in Frederick, Colorado, for a few great days in 2016 that helped us prepare for our craft beer journey.

My group text thread: Jeff Hoffman, Mike Soderlind, Steve Brown, Chris Strickland, John Lark Herron, and Derek Barney. Always good for laughs while I'm trying to do work.

Other friends and fellow Pensacolians who have impacted our lives and business in a positive way: Michelle MacNeil, J.P. MacNeil, Samba Johnson, Kevin Krieger, Lumon May, Daniela De Castro, Mayor Grover Robinson, Michelle Salzman, Scott Remington, Steve Schale, Chad Henderson, Travis Peterson, Joe and Suzannah Driver, Alex Andrade, Jon Shell, Jayer Williamson, Will Dunaway, Dylan

Nadsady, Bruce Vredenburg, Adam Roth and his band Grizfolk, Keith Hoskins, Bob Anderson, and Jason and Sarah Blaydes.

Sam Calagione of Dogfish Head, Jeffrey Stuffings of Jester King, Audra Gaiziunas of Bhramari, Doug Reiser of Burial, Bart Watson of the Brewers Association, Nic Pelaez, Director of Hospitality at Modern Times Beer Co., and Matthew Stevens and David Stein of Creature Comforts for your time and contributions to this book to help breweries nationwide.

Chapter 1
Before You Begin

THIS IDEA BEGAN on Church Street in Asheville, North Carolina, in 2015. I realize the irony of this specific street locale, probably as some kind of Freudian nod to the higher power we needed to see us through on this journey.

My business partner, Reed Odeneal, the brewing operations expert in our two-man team, lived there at the time and we were *actually* exploring opening a brewery, this thing that we used to joke about as co-workers a few years earlier that we both knew would never come to fruition.

Except now it might. Or at least we were meeting to talk about it. A shift in my job responsibilities in Pensacola, Florida, was pending, and while my job wasn't in jeopardy, it was enough of a spark in timing to give this wild idea the smell test. I had returned to Pensacola, my hometown, about a year before, and I knew if I were ever going to do this, our best chance to be successful would be in this market that I knew well and knew was undersaturated compared to the burgeoning craft beer industry happening nationwide.

He was smart, with a professional background in IT and tons of homebrewing experience. I had grown up around business in my family and spent more than a decade in journalism, bringing at least a decent understanding of branding, communication, and marketing as well as some connections and credibility with local investors. Neither of us had ever opened our own business before.

But we texted about it. We split up some research for a few weeks. I texted back one day in November 2015 and wrote, "Let's open this brewery and just say f**k it." (I never said I was measured.)

I bought a plane ticket on a whim and flew up to Asheville. Worst case was a solid excuse for a couple days drinking beer in Asheville.

1

We were at Reed's apartment on Church Street in a quiet living room save for the claws of two ill-behaved dachshunds scampering across the hardwood floor.

Every few minutes, one of us blurted out something we found online, or a calculation for how much we thought our power bill would be to brew a 10-barrel batch, or a cool photo of a brewery we liked.

I remember a particular moment in this research. I came across a blog from a brewery (I forget which one), where they wrote this long, flowery post about their two-year voyage from starting the idea of a brewery to their grand opening. The trying times, the reward of getting it done, the sacrifices, all of that.

"Two years – what took them so long?" I remember asking out loud, both rhetorically and naively. "They must not have known what they were doing."

Neither did we.

So exactly two years and fifteen days later, Reed and I opened Perfect Plain Brewing Company in an old 5,400-square-foot print shop we purchased in downtown Pensacola. We learned a lot in those two years and fifteen days.

REED ODENEAL (left) and D.C. Reeves after spending a week making beer at Echo Brewing Co. in Frederick, Colorado. We're smiling because we didn't know how much we had in front of us yet.

Humility, for instance.

Patience, too.

So many more things I can't wait to share with you in this book.

And I'll jump ahead, but we became one of Florida's busiest tap-rooms in our first year of operation and were among the top quartile in taproom beer production in spite of the fact that we distributed zero barrels. For us, that was a large accomplishment. We are tucked far from Florida's major population hubs. A town of less than 100,000, Pensacola is buried in the far northwest tip of Florida, just 10 miles from the Alabama state line. Our job was both quality and consumer beer education in this market, and all while doing things like making beer styles that had not been made here before and doing new things like our city's first-ever bottle release. We were fortunate enough to beat our Year 1 revenue projection by 74 percent.

In Year 2, completed a $400,000 expansion into an outdoor space and private event venue in a former horse stable while working on a second expansion to create the city's finest cocktail bar and the city's firstever barrel room.

I'm writing the *Microbrewery Handbook* so we can share everything we learned about becoming brewery owners, and more specifically, entrepreneurs in the constantly evolving craft beer business. I hope this handbook is impactful, that it saves you from missteps, and it puts you in a position to thrive while sharing your beer and your heart with your community.

For those homebrewers and daydreaming entrepreneurs whose minds wander in their cubicle like mine did a few years ago, this book should lay the groundwork for all the other stuff that lifts your beer above the rest.

I don't want to scare you – you can do this. And your chances of success should increase after reading this book. I wish I would have had a book to help guide us through some of this in 2015.

For breweries, cideries, vineyards, or craft beer bars in planning, this should be a reference for you on your desk during these crucial months. And for breweries or bars already established, we share some of our implementable secrets that have helped us master employee engagement, company culture, a strong brand, and what we see as a bright future.

The craft beer market is evolving rapidly, maybe even more than you realize. And what we're seeing in 2019 is a plateau on the overall craft market. What seemed to be an invincible business model even four to five years ago – hundreds of breweries of all sizes and formats opening and a mere handful closing nationwide – has sharpened.

Competition, likely around you and where you hope to begin or grow your brewery, has sharpened as well.

In November of 2018 the Brewers Association even created a new "Taproom" class of brewers to go with Packaging Breweries and Pub Breweries. This is a class that serves more than 25 percent of its product on site with minimal food operations and that produces fewer than six million barrels per year.

It's like anything else in business. People see a trend that's successful, and the market saturates. Add that to the fact that this is beer we're talking about here – a fun industry in the grand scheme of life – and you find the market where it is now.

Dogfish Head Brewing Founder Sam Calagione said it best in 2018 when he lovingly summarized the evolving craft beer market as a "phenomenon I'll call smiling mouth, jaws of death."

He explained that there are two jaws that represent different strong sectors of the current craft beer market: taproom-focused models and the other side of the coin, "fairly scaled" breweries that are doing multi-state distribution. He advised not to get stuck in between those two models as our industry evolves.

"The bottom jaw, frankly, is more of those taproom-oriented breweries that can kick ass because they're in control of their sales and they can get so much margin by selling across the bar," he said. "So many of those business units, if they have quality, consistency, are well differentiated and focused, they're going to weather this storm with grace and aplomb."

This book centers around that bottom jaw of the industry that we've created at Perfect Plain. Amazingly, while other distribution-based sectors of craft plateau or fall, 15 percent of all draft beer sales in the U.S. were sold direct from breweries in 2018, according to the Brewers Association – an all-time high.

My hope is that the *Microbrewery Handbook* will give you the entire toolkit you need to kick ass as a brewery focused on a hyper-local taproom first and foremost – the place I believe is the most prudent and impactful to start in this industry today.

During the Florida Brewers Guild Conference in 2017, Sam Adams Founder Jim Koch told the audience that if he were opening Sam Adams today, he would do it as a taproom-focused model.

This book focuses on the construction and refinement of your entire microbrewery organization from start to finish, from planning, strategy, financing, and permitting to common pitfalls, employee culture, and best practices.

We're going to cover a lot of ground here.

To find some focus, I spent a week in Nashville to write this book, and when people asked me what I was doing in town, I would elevator-pitch the topic of my book this way: If you know how to make great beer, or you're already making great beer, my book is covering everything else it takes to start or grow a successful microbrewery.

This microbrewery book will not spend a lot of time focusing on the beer itself. I know – great beer is why we got into this business, right? It's what we're passionate about. Even though I'm not a professional brewer, I would never have opened any type of business other than a craft brewery. I'm a craft beer fan and love so much about the industry and how it has impacted communities. I would have never opened it anywhere other than my hometown.

There are plenty of product-focused books written by people who have forgotten more than I know about the creation of beer. If you are looking for the perfect imperial stout grain bill or techniques on rectifying a stuck mash, this is not your book.

However, we will talk some about sizing up your system for success and the marriage between a successful operation and the ability it gives you to add muscle to your long-term beer quality and offerings.

But even if you don't own a brewery yourself yet, as the craft industry populates (and let's not even get into the invasion of craft spirits), I can guarantee you one thing: Every day that goes by in this industry means that more of the success of a brewery will be predicated on who can do all of the other stuff well.

"I think there's definitely more interest in talking about the business of beer," Jester King Founder Jeffrey Stuffings told me earlier this year. "I definitely do feel it's less of a taboo subject (than in years past). When we started doing stuff like this, I personally felt, like, 'Oh man, maybe I'm kind of selling out here. Maybe I'm starting to be the man, whatever.'

"And now, I just don't feel that. I think it's responsible to be doing these things and having these conversations."

Who can create a differentiating customer experience? Who will spend the time to understand permitting, buildout, and how to avoid construction pitfalls? Who can make their place a great one to work and treat their employees like they're owners? Who can learn to hire brewers and bartenders brilliantly using the same process that major hospital systems use to hire their CEOs? Who is willing to drop their ego to do the right thing for the organization and its employees? Who will use measurable achievement to make sure the organization is on track? Who will use their social media and branding consistently and optimally to build the company's image the right way?

In the book *E-Myth Revisited: Why Most Small Businesses Don't Work and What to Do About It,* author Michael Gerber explains how the vast majority of small businesses in our nation are opened by "technicians." That means the baker opens the bakery. The chef opens the restaurant. The brewer opens the brewery. It's the natural progression of someone looking to use their passion for bigger reward and satisfaction.

But if you can separate yourself from the love of brewing for a moment, the truth is that the technical skill to bake a great wedding cake or cook perfect escargot or develop a delicious hazy IPA, in the grand scheme of small business, is likely a much smaller piece of the pie than you think. The problem is, many technicians don't realize this until it's too late. They focus so much on the technical that they lose sight of everything around them. Or they don't see pitfalls coming. Or in some cases, ego gets in the way of sound decision making.

Don't get me wrong; there is a litany of major success stories, like Calagione himself, of technicians opening amazing breweries. Tons of them. But in many cases, including Dogfish Head, breweries make smart business decisions based on market conditions and surround themselves with a great team and the knowledge to run a craft beer business, not just brew beer.

Gerber's book also talks about the massive difference in success of a franchise company against a single-chain small business. Why? Because of the structure. The standard operating procedures. Those are baked in from the start, and that illustrates how important this other non-beer stuff is.

Here is a sample of common mistakes I've seen with closed and struggling breweries around the nation:

1. Overspending on equipment and underspending on your taproom.
2. Poor employee culture and customer service because they're treated like an afterthought to beer.
3. Ego dictating important decisions like the mix of styles on a tap list or the idea that a brewery's differentiator in a market will be "We're going to make the best beer." (Don't we ALL think that?!)

4. The inability to delegate important parts of your company – I call this "not finding the right seats on the bus."
5. Lack of preparation on the brewery organization outside of brewing equipment and brewery design.

If you are a brewer who is pursuing your dream to open your own place, you've come to the right place. I'm here to equip and prepare you for your experience moving from mere technician to part technician, part entrepreneur. I consider the most important part of Perfect Plain's early success to be that Reed and I balanced each other, trusted each other, and were self-aware of our strengths and weaknesses.

I'm writing this book not only because we were able to open a microbrewery successfully, but because we've done it *recently*. In this craft beer climate. And while there are so many great resources out there in this industry, at the pace it evolves now, I feel sharing this recent experience can prove more bountiful in your quest.

In my previous life, before I put every cent I had into Perfect Plain, I spent fifteen years as a journalist covering college football at Florida State University and the University of Alabama. All those road trips and taproom Friday nights all over the South nurtured my love for craft. And whatever sliver of journalist brain survived when I left the business meant that throughout our two years and fifteen days of preparation to open PPBC, I kept good notes and remembered things that impacted us the most, and hurt the most, and all the things I would write about if I were to ever tell our story. The stories I would want to make sure I tell prospective business owners before they take the leap.

So, let's be clear: If you are reading this book, I'm making an assumption about you. I'm assuming that you and your team are committed to high-quality and consistent product that you're proud to serve. Or that you're committed to hiring the right person who knows how to do this for you. This is, of course, vital for success. I can't help you sell terrible beer. We all know that the saturation of the market has brought us great beer. It's also brought us some bad beer that we are all concerned will taint new craft consumers.

We're going to work on the rest of the pie, one that was once optional in this space several years ago. Today, growing your brewery into a healthy organization that makes beer is an absolute must.

Chapter 2

How to Use This Book

THESE PAGES AHEAD outline our learning experience opening Perfect Plain Brewing Company in Pensacola, Florida, a 10-barrel taproom-focused company that took more than two years of planning, coffee, learning, beer, anxiety, mentors, excitement, luck, and hard work to open our doors on November 21, 2017.

What I hope to provide in this book, oddly, reminds me so much of my own interesting experience when I was 15 and learning how to drive a car with a manual transmission. People younger than 30 may be unfamiliar with such a term.

In 2000 I had saved up $1,800 from summer restaurant jobs to buy my first car. I made the crucial first mistake of allowing resident master negotiator and my father, Jim Reeves, to actually do the vehicle purchasing.

Dad calls one afternoon and says he has my first car, and as the suspense builds and my enthusiasm overflows, around the corner comes a black 1991 Toyota Tercel hatchback. This is the precise vehicle you buy when you have absolutely no concern about whether high school girls will find you attractive. Torn seats. Busted shocks. The tires could probably be fitted to a riding lawnmower, and in case I ever expected to arrive at social gatherings with any semblance of suave, my muffler sputtered loudly for what felt like minutes *after* the car ignition was cut.

Today, I rationalize this to simple "character building."

So Day 1 in the Tercel was a lesson from Jim on how to drive a stick shift. I had zero days' experience; my father, who was already 62 at the time, knew manual transmission for the majority of his life.

The lesson began with spins around his office parking lot. It did not go well.

He was unconsciously competent. He had done this for so long and had learned how to do this so long ago, that it just came naturally to him. Probably like mashing in or bartending for many of us today. Problem is, for many who reach that level of competence, you just might stink when it comes to teaching people who are consciously *incompetent*. I was consciously incompetent. I was conscious very early, likely after the first whiplash-inducing stall, that I had no idea what I was doing. My father was equally bad at communicating a sound strategy for success. Conceptually, this is why Michael Jordan, the best basketball player of all time, would probably struggle as an NBA head coach while his significantly less heralded Chicago Bulls teammate in the early 1990s, Steve Kerr, is considered perhaps the best coach in the NBA. Jordan played at too high a level. He was too good even to remember how to teach a rookie about the intricacies of cracking the roster at the NBA level.

So, after that first driving debacle, a classmate of mine, Allie Gessler, taught me how to drive a stick shift in 10 minutes. I had it. Allie, of approximately eight months of legal driving experience, was able to clearly explain what I was doing wrong and identify what I didn't know. Why? Because she had learned recently herself. She had felt her own whiplash pain and remembered how to stop it. In the midst of just telling me to take my foot off the clutch and onto the gas, my Dad left out the subtleties, like *slowly take your foot off the clutch as you add to the gas, like they're tied together on a string.*

As someone who just opened a taproom-focused microbrewery two years ago, I hope to be that guide for you. The one who remembers the granular yet vital parts of starting their own microbrewery because we've recently done it ourselves. We've done it in this ever-changing, saturating, and evolving market of craft beer where growth has started to plateau and the strategy for success looks wildly different from how it would have even six or seven years ago.

Perfect Plain Brewing Company has been quickly successful beyond our expectations, for which I'm so thankful. Reed and I were prepared. And I think our company and its foundational culture is built around some exceptional things that any brewery, new or old, regardless of size, could install to create a better place to work and a better place for customers to enjoy. We have advantages and some unique ways of doing things that I'm so excited to share with the craft beer world.

My hope is the sheer freshness and recency of my journey of opening a craft brewery, coupled with my coincidentally convenient background as a reporter who reports to nice readers like you, means that our hard lessons and our breakthrough successes prove beneficial for you.

There are so many great, experienced and brilliant minds in the craft brewing business, and that fact makes me proud just to say I'm in the same world. I'm both fortunate and grateful that some of those incredible minds were willing to contribute their thoughts and experiences in these pages to help others achieve their goals. I learned so much from them as they shared their valuable time.

We'll talk about the value of a taproom, about financing, about partners, about tough lessons learned and potential hurdles in your quest to start your dream.

When we called this a handbook, we meant it.

This book can be read front to back, but it can be used just as effectively as a quick referral guide. You can read up on or refer to specific topics that you hope to learn about or improve.

In addition, you'll find a robust reference guide and a website, www.microbreweryhandbook.com, that will include some templates and documents I refer to throughout the book that you are welcome to utilize in your business.

Some chapters have a deeper dive; others are fast-paced and bulleted. The goal isn't a rambling novel, but a practical and memorable guide to create and grow your own success. The goal isn't to go mind-numbingly deep, but to inform well and spark additional research if needed.

You should be able to find value in these pages regardless of whether you're just a home brewer daydreaming of opening your own place or you're already a successful microbrewery owner looking to make some improvements.

Collaboration, sharing and striving to create a quality product are what make our industry so great.

By the way, while you'll hear me mention breweries the most, the overwhelming majority of this book also translates to opening a cidery, a distillery, a kombucha bar, and so on. The principles of creating a great place to work, understanding projections, setting goals, and marketing your brand can cross all of those avenues, no matter what you're manufacturing in the back.

In addition, I was fortunate enough to have an amazing list of people sit down with me and share their thoughts about the industry, their successes, and even some of their mistakes.

In these pages you will get thoughts from Dogfish President Sam Calagione, Jester King Founder Jeffrey Stuffings, Brewers Association Chief Economist Bart Watson, Modern Times Director of Hospitality Nic Pelaez, Burial Beer Co. Co-Founder Doug Reiser, and Bhramari Brewing CEO Audra Gaiziunas. You'll also hear from Quint Studer, the founder of the nation's top healthcare consulting company, Studer Group. He has been credited as the pioneer of cultivating a high level of customer service in the healthcare space, much of which has translated to the craft beer world at Perfect Plain.

Let's let off the clutch and get started.

Part I
The Basics

LET'S LAY THE groundwork.

Before a tactical deep dive on how to make this microbrewery dream a reality, we'll attack some of the overarching beer topics, including the state of the ever-evolving craft beer industry with Brewers Association Chief Economist Bart Watson, the pure power of the craft beer taproom in today's industry, and a key that translates to any brewery in any region in any format: how to differentiate yourself.

Our friend Sam Calagione of Dogfish Head was even gracious enough to share his thoughts with us about the industry, its future and how to be welldifferentiated.

This foundation will help any brewery hone its scope and get going down the right path to success.

Chapter 3
State of the Industry – for Now

WE'VE ALL BEEN witness to a surge in interest in craft beer in the past decade. The numbers have exploded.

Its growth has become well known in the mainstream, with numbers from the Brewers Association backing up what we all feel and see happening: The BA reports there were 7,485 craft breweries open in the United States in 2018, an explosion of historic proportions. That's triple the amount from just six years prior (2,475 in 2012), and *more than 10 times* as many as there were 25 years ago.

I'd like to be able to give you, at the precise moment you read this sentence, a perfectly accurate assessment of the craft beer industry. But as most industries, it's ever evolving.

In a market that has grown as rapidly as craft beer has, even in the past eight to ten years, where the market goes from here is a big question – a question that any brewery, cidery, winery, or distillery should be asking itself.

What we all know well is that, over the past ten to fifteen years, craft beer has enjoyed a renaissance. We also know that the rate of breweries opening to closing in the U.S. has remained strong, although we've seen the number of closings start their uptick.

After years of double-digit year-over-year growth, the pace has slowed in 2017 and 2018. As the chart shows, the craft beer market grew less than 4 percent in 2018, according to Brewers Association Chief Economist Bart Watson.

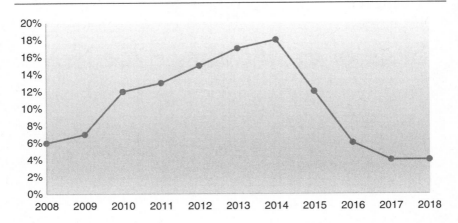

"Whether you see the market as mature or not is now a factor of geography and business model. If you're a widely distributed production brewery in Portland, Denver, or San Diego, you probably see a pretty mature market," Watson wrote in April of 2019. "If you're a taproom brewer in Birmingham, Little Rock or Lexington, you probably see more run room.

"Regardless, I'd advise all breweries to think about the future more as one where craft grows in line with overall economic growth rather than expecting a return to the golden decade we've just experienced."

The slowing of growth can be looked at in different ways. Watson, for example, pointed out that the small growth in 2018 still was almost 1,000,000 more craft beer barrels produced than the year prior. Craft beer sales by dollar rose 7 percent year over year as well. Best yet, craft beer now has a 13.2 percent market share when it was once thought impossible for craft to ever breach the 10 percent mark against the big-beer conglomerates. Some version of a slowdown is obvious, but it may not necessarily signal a downturn, more of a fast rise and saturation of the market starting to take hold, causing the slowed trajectory of what was almost unprecedented growth.

It's also fair to point out that standing up a brewery, as you may know all too well, is not a quick process. So that means there are still people in the process of opening breweries that began a year ago or longer, so even the slowing pace of opening breweries will have some inertia when it does slow down.

Watson is not the only one predicting some version of a craft beer speed trap. To expect massive growth to continue at the pace we've seen is unattainable. As with any market that saturates, the truth is that opening a brewery today takes much more thought, planning, leadership, and organizational culture combined to create a truly great craft beer experience. Hopefully this book and our experiences can help out with a few of those things.

So what does that mean for you? I think it means, to Watson's point, that gone are the days of being automatically successful because you are the only brewery in town. There was once a time when craft brewing was a novel idea and the first to market in a community – or heck, even a region – was good enough to get people through your doors. Experience and beer quality were secondary. Today, there's too much competition for that. What was once a novelty – to drink beer made in the same room you're sitting in – has now become a marketplace where the consumer is becoming more educated about options, and making "local beer" can't stand on its own.

How you market, how you build relationships, how you lead your organization – not just how you operate your brewhouse – matters more now than ever.

I asked Watson in mid-2019 about what market-based metrics he sees as most important to track when deciding to open your craft brewery.

"I'd certainly be looking at how many other breweries there are, and this isn't as simple as you saying, 'If there's no breweries, great, and if there's a ton of breweries, bad.' I think there is the sweet spot somewhere in the middle where you've shown that there's a market opportunity," Watson said. "Maybe in my market people like small breweries, they like going to them, but this isn't Portland or Denver yet (in terms of market saturation). So, looking at the number of breweries, I'd be looking at how breweries that opened a couple of years ago are doing, not just the ones who just opened, but let's look at breweries that are three or four years old. Are they still finding growth opportunities in the marketplace?

"I would be looking at what styles are selling relative to the business model that I'm building as well."

What I take away from my own observations and Watson's comments is that the window of a half-hearted leap into this industry because its "a hot market" has closed. If you're getting in, you must be passionate, prepared and wellcapitalized to set yourself apart from the competition.

Additional threats aren't just from the brewery down the street. Craft spirits, cideries, and distillery taprooms have become more and more prominent. The increase of legalization and access to cannabis could play a role presently and in the future. Watson also believes that both regulatory pushback and "brewery experience" imitation from traditional bar/restaurants will continue to grow as those markets have seen the meteoric rise of craft.

"It's hard to predict the twists and turns this crazy industry takes," Watson said when I asked him to make some bold craft beer predictions for 2022. "I think we'll be talking a little bit less about kind of the crazy new product innovation. I think that we're starting to see that swing back a little bit already and people are going to be looking.

"I think that we're going to see craft demographic age a little bit. . .. So the people who are in their mid- to late 20s now are going to be in their early to mid-30s, and the people in their 30s will be in their 40s, and people will be a little bit more fixed in their preferences and maybe be seeking variety a little bit less.

"From the taproom perspective, I think that the service quality is only going to get more and more important, but that a lot of people are going to be thinking about how to balance that quality with rising labor costs. That's certainly, I think, going to be a challenge for a lot of breweries. I wouldn't be surprised to see more minimum wage laws in a whole bunch of states, and that will put pressure on what admittedly now is heavily a service that's not just a manufacturing business."

Watson highlighted some other trends he expects to see in the future, including the standard bar mutating itself to be more like a craft brewery.

"I think we're going to see brewers get pushback from retail, not just regulatory-wise but competition-wise. I think you're going to see a lot of retailers starting to adopt the things that have made taprooms successful," he said. "So brewers are going to be looking at ways that they are really enhancing the brewery side of their experience to remind people that they can do things that other restaurants and bars that are kind of copying their model can't do. I think you're going to see a whole spate of retailers that build out and look a lot like the generic taproom."

This is in no way to scare you away from opening or ramping up a craft brewery. Under that logic, why is anyone opening a conventional bar or restaurant anymore – aren't there a lot of those in the world? It's important to know the landscape and to highlight the ever-increasing importance to differentiate yourself from the competition that is getting wider and stronger each day.

Don't count on the novelty of creating local beer alone.

Chapter Homework: Test Your Market

- Anyone opening a business in any industry should have a full understanding of the world around them. Are there a lot of breweries or cideries? Are you the first one to market? Even if for some wild reason you weren't interested in doing this research, rest assured that any bank or lending institution is going to want to see your assessment of the competition. It's okay if there are other breweries around. But do they do the same things you are doing? In later chapters we'll talk more about "differentiators" to set a brewery apart.

In fact, we had to explain to several lenders in our Pensacola market that there are cities that have more than just one or two breweries. Be prepared to have a firm understanding of who's around, what they do, and what you're going to do different or better.

You can build the best taproom and serve the best beer in your state. But if you spend $1.5 million to build it out, and 4,000 people live in your town in Nowhere, South Dakota, you are extremely less likely to be successful. Don't be blinded by what you think you want to do. Be sure to vet your market objectively.

Websites for More Information on the State of the Industry

Brewers Association: www.BrewersAssociation.org

Brewbound: www.Brewbound.com

CraftBeer.com: www.craftbeer.com

CraftBrewingBusiness.com www.craftbrewingbusiness.com

Chapter 4

Focus on Your Taproom First

LET'S TALK ABOUT Sam Calagione's "bottom jaw" analogy and why he believes the taproom model will survive the continued saturation of the craft beer industry. It comes down to a simple understanding of the distinct financial advantage of your taproom.

As states around the U.S. have continued to modernize legislation to allow for this amazing interaction that we all love – bringing consumers straight to the source of your product – the taproom model has emerged as the strongest and safest way to make a brewery successful.

Nothing in business is guaranteed. You aren't gifted profitability and success by merely opening a taproom. That becomes truer by the minute as more people enter this market. We'll cover some of those things throughout the book.

According to the Brewers Association, as of 2019, these are the top three reasons why people visit taprooms:

1. They want to sample different beers.
2. They want to learn about the beers.
3. They know it will be fresh.

Few bars can replicate this the way a taproom can. This model has an ability to create a localized, immersive experience that assumes peak freshness and that authentic fascination of sipping at the site of manufacture. It also assumes the expertise on beer that your taproom can provide.

Talk about some builtin advantages!

It's such a successful model that Bart Watson of the Brewers Association mentioned one emerging trend we're seeing more in the more saturated markets. Outside companies are opening beer bars with the same taproom vibe as a brewery but instead of brewing their own beer they curate a craft beer list, blurring the line of creating that taproom experience without the true manufacturing element. Imitation is the sincerest form of flattery, right?

"When people talk about a slow down or plateau in the craft beer market, I make it pretty clear that you need to separate out distribution models from the taproom models," Watson said. "We are seeing a slowdown in the former, but we're really not seeing things slow in the latter.

"The taproom business model is about half the growth in craft right now. We're seeing that model be popular and be profitable – so much so that larger craft breweries and other companies are starting to pivot into that model."

The model continues to emerge. According to the Alcohol and Tobacco Tax and Trade Bureau, almost 75 percent of breweries in the U.S. are producing fewer than 1,000 barrels of beer annually.

Inside the Numbers

Let's talk numbers behind the evolution of the taproom model. Ask any financial advisor or accountant – doesn't matter if they know beer or not – the taproom edge boils down to one vital figure: an extremely strong gross margin. That means by the time you add up your *cost of goods sold* (in essence, your direct costs to manufacture the beer, such as power, natural gas, brewing labor, hops, yeast, grain, CO_2, fruit, etc.) and compare that to the top line revenue – total dollars – made off that beer, by serving those beers directly to your consumer, $1,000 per barrel or more in top-line sales is comfortably attainable in the taproom. In distribution, it's impossible.

One of the most popular questions I get from customers now is "So are you guys distributing?"

So their eyes don't glaze over, I've concocted a concise explanation that goes something like this: The taproom model in Florida cuts out not just *the* middle man; it cuts out **two** middle men. First, a distributor in our area is looking for a 28–30 percent markup. Then, that distributor is going to turn around and sell that beer to a restaurant or a bar, which will be looking for a 350–400 percent markup.

	Taproom Sales	Distribution Sales
Revenue per half-barrel	$575–650	$135–160
Revenue per 10 BBL batch	$11,500–$13,000	$2,700–$3,200

You sell a half-barrel for $140 to a distributor. That distributor gets its 30 percent margin then turns and sells it to a bar for $182. Factoring for spillage, the bar gets 110 pints out of that half-barrel, they sell your pints for $5.75, and that keg top lines at $632.50. Sound like a lot of money to make on one keg?

Well, you can make *more*.

Simply put, would you rather make kegs for $60–80 (at our scale, this varies on brewery sizing, ingredients, etc.) and sell a lot at $140? Or does fewer kegs at $632.50 sound better?

If I want to grow my business in a healthy way, with cash flow and ability to pay down debt service, I like the $632.50 option.

"The taproom model is the easiest way to prove your concepts, but it is also the least amount of risk to take financially," said Audra Gaiziunas, CEO of Asheville, North Carolina, Bhramari Brewing and founder of Brewed For Her Ledger, an accounting firm focused specifically on breweries. "You're going to gain your investment back. Your payback period is going to be shortest that way, but it also involves the least amount of risk. If you need to get more cash to the drawer, bring more people to the taproom."

Perfect Plain is a 10-barrel brewhouse, making anywhere from 16–20 half-barrel kegs per batch depending on style and efficiency. I spitball estimate that each 12-ounce pour costs us 50–60 cents to make, and the larger the brewhouse a brewery has, the lower that number goes. Our average price in the taproom is $6 for 12 ounces, including sales tax. While startup costs are high, no bar can replicate that gross margin.

This single point has changed the craft beer game, and it's absolutely vital that anyone opening a brewery understands this point. There is no distribution-first model that can ever reap this kind of potential reward as quickly. Can you be successful in distribution? Sure. But just Google "brewery closings" and there is a common thread. Most were either: 1) breweries looking to break into the market only through distribution first, spending little to no money or time on taproom presence, or 2) undercapitalized breweries that may have found early success through a taproom, but doubled down in distribution, investing too many resources into an area where the profit margin pales in comparison. Translation: They moved too fast without understanding their market and sunk too much into a business model that couldn't sustain.

Value of a Taproom-First Model

If I haven't convinced you yet, let's talk about some other reasons to focus on your taproom first. There's a reason it's growing faster than any other sector in craft beer.

- It builds your brand. If you ever do make the leap to distribution, it's nice to have a strong reputation instead of jumping in head first.
- It allows you to experiment and determine what beers consumers would like when you do decide to distribute.
- All the awesome things you want to do. An expanded sour and/or barrel program? An expansion? More marketing, better taproom space, more staff, and more dollars for training and development?

Talking about the financials of a brewery can sometimes feel taboo because of our industry's authenticity and passion for its product. I know that talking money in this business that was built on creativity and the art of craft can rub some the wrong way. As someone who came into this industry as a craft beer fan and not a professional brewer, I sometimes feel prejudged as someone who didn't enter this business from the technical side. But it's all about how you position this data.

Let me tell you what being profitable and being successful means. It cultivates so many positive impacts outside of your own pocket. When you make more money, and your taproom is busy, that creates jobs in your community. All of our bartenders made $30–$35 an hour in 2018, which in our smaller Pensacola market would put them significantly above the income average, regardless of profession. That's helping a dozen families put food on their table, and helps support and give a great life to our three collective daughters our company has in those families.

I take responsibility for more than a dozen employees and their quality of life. I'm motivated to keep our taproom busy so they can pay rent, support children and spouses and dogs and cats, and ultimately be proud to say they work for our company.

Even as our company cash flowed immediately and beat our projections, as I type this in early 2019, more than a year after we opened, ownership hasn't taken a dime out of the company. Instead, we've reinvested every cent we've made. We bought a foeder and launched a to-go bottle program. We're undergoing an expansion to create a beer garden, a private event space, a barrel room, and a new lab for our brewing operations. We bought a food trailer.

We've made improvements in beer quality, processing, customer experience, and employee experience. Those are all things we can get behind, and those are all things that take cash flow to make happen.

Financial conversations in your brewery shouldn't be taboo. When you focus on your taproom, the financial engine to make your brewery successful, you should look at it as the fastest way to ramp up your quality, your community engagement, and your brand.

Let me be clear: This is not me suggesting you should *never* distribute. In fact, at the time I'm writing this, Perfect Plain is looking to invest in its own distribution company. For the moment, Florida's three-tier distribution system is immensely one-sided against craft beer – lifetime contracts with very few avenues to keep distributors accountable – but while there has been an annual push to loosen those archaic rules, there is a law that allows a brewery to have passive ownership in a distribution company for up to eight years.

We are exploring that, but we are keeping clear focus on our primary revenue stream: taproom sales. So, the term for what we are pursuing is lovably called "billboard distribution." It means that as a 10-barrel brewing facility, we have no desire at this time to just put our beer anywhere. We're wanting to be meticulous about its location so it is more likely to lead to draft sales at the taproom.

We're fueling the engines. We're picking bars and restaurants that we feel fit our brand, and our model, and our target customers. That way, we know that because we were exclusive to those particular businesses, and they know we aren't just at any bar, they will do a great job presenting, showcasing, and upselling our beer as well as guide customers our way.

The irony here is that at our scale, this billboard distribution will *not* be a money maker for us. I am researching ways to minimize our expenses in hopes of just breaking even. Maybe we move just 20–30 barrels a month to handselected accounts? Can we do that, hire someone, lease a cold room space, and buy a truck and not lose our shirt doing it? Likely not.

However, I'm willing to make this distribution format a loss leader for the company with the goal of increasing taproom sales and brand identity.

What I want is that restaurant customer to ask for a local beer, drink our Holy Spin IPA, ask about our brewery, and have that waiter tell them we're a few blocks away with 20 beers on tap and in bottles. Hopefully he or she throws in that our taproom is cool and fun.

There are ways to make money in distribution, but that's not my forte. They are out there. But as you'll learn, the margin is tighter, the risk of failure is higher, and the industry influx will be taking out distribution taps first.

Chapter Homework: Be Thinking About Your Plans for These Three Things

1. **Up-front capital.** Bear in mind, to obtain that strong gross margin, the downside is that the price of entry into the craft beer business is steep. It's the startup cost of equipment, a building, and/or a long-term lease. (Do whatever you can to buy or have a future option to buy your building – more on this later.) Simply put, to get that excellent gross margin by making your own beer, you're paying some up-front costs. But if you're smart about those up-front costs, you can reap the rewards of a great margin in perpetuity (unless you undersize your brewery equipment dramatically, and that's for another chapter).

2. **Location, location, location.** You can make the best beer in your community and it will have a fraction of the impact on your sales that your location will. You need to seek foot traffic. Sure, one of the great things about the craft beer business is that our target consumer is more likely to seek us out as a destination compared to a standard bar. Just because that's true doesn't mean you should

skimp on added cost for a prime location. This is especially the case if you already have craft breweries succeeding in walkable and high-trafficked parts of your downtown core. Saving a little on a lease payment won't make or break your business. Location will make or break your business.

3. **Commitment to taproom.** Don't overlook the expenses of creating a great taproom. Have good furniture and fixtures. Good doesn't mean expensive; it just means if you can afford a $300,000 10-barrel turnkey brewing system, you shouldn't have your taproom look like a mismatched thrift store. We see this quite often in our travels around the country. We invested more money in our taproom than we did our equipment. We can always grow into and upgrade equipment. It's much, much more difficult to pick up and move a taproom or overcome a lacking first impression if your taproom isn't up to par when you open.

The Four Market Segments, According to the Brewers Association

Microbrewery
A brewery that produces fewer than 15,000 barrels (17,600 hectoliters) of beer per year, with 75 percent or more of its beer sold off-site. Microbreweries sell to the public by one or more of the following methods: the traditional three-tier system (brewer to wholesaler to retailer to consumer); the two-tier system (brewer acting as wholesaler to retailer to consumer); and directly to the consumer through carryouts and/or on-site taproom or restaurant sales.

Brewpub
A restaurant-brewery that sells 25 percent or more of its beer onsite. The beer is brewed primarily for sale in the restaurant and bar. The beer is often dispensed directly from the brewery's storage tanks. Where allowed by law, brewpubs often sell beer "to go" and/or distribute to off-site accounts. Note: BA recategorizes a company as a microbrewery if its off-site (distributed) beer sales exceed 75 percent.

Contract Brewing Company
A business that hires another brewery to produce its beer. It can also be a brewery that hires another brewery to produce additional beer. The contract brewing company handles marketing, sales, and distribution of its beer, while generally leaving the brewing and packaging to its producer-brewery (which, confusingly, is also sometimes referred to as a contract brewery).

Regional Craft Brewery
An independent regional brewery with a majority of volume in "traditional" or "innovative" beer(s).

Source: Brewers Association.

Chapter 5
How to Differentiate
Your Brewery

ONE OF MY favorite things about opening Perfect Plain is being able to help others follow their dream of opening their own business.

It's why this book exists, and I continue both to help and to learn from new entrepreneurs every day.

When someone asks me to meet with them to discuss their idea, I open with a warning. I tell them that I'm going to be asking them questions as if they were asking me today to invest in their company. I understand their idea or their projections or other considerations may not be fully developed. However, I feel that qualifier allows me to ask questions without the person feeling as if they aren't adequate to open a business. And if they can't answer some of the questions I have, it gives that person some homework to work on. But they know my line of questioning comes from a place that's helpful, not off-putting or judgmental.

After I hear about their idea, its strengths, their passion for the project, and why they believe it can succeed, I always begin my inquisition around how much research has been done in their market. One recent meeting was about opening a coffee shop downtown. About six years ago, there was one coffee shop. There are now five with more on the way, and some great ones. Now a Starbucks, which had never been downtown at all, has moved in close by. This is thematic in Pensacola; we've seen a renaissance in the past half-decade thanks to private downtown development, rich history – it is America's first settlement – and sugar-white beaches on the Gulf of Mexico. Pensacola was just named one of National Geographic's 30 best cities in America for 2019.

So my question was this: *There are already five here, and more on the way. What will you be doing differently?*

If I were investing in the sixth coffee shop of a relatively small downtown, I would *have* to feel comfortable knowing we had something no one else could replicate, at least easily. The best location by far? The best space by far? The coolest vibe? Baristas who were sent to harvest the beans from Africa with their own bare hands? Something. And who knows, this sixth shop could become nationally renowned for coffee down the road.

He didn't have an answer for that quite yet, and wasn't far along, but hopefully it gave him something to think about.

Why not be the first mobile coffee shop in Pensacola? That's a differentiator. Not only do we have a beach that would be ripe for this kind of business before early morning walks in the sand, but we have a huge running and biking culture and are home to marathons, 5Ks, and triathlons almost every weekend. We have massive arts and seafood festivals – so many revenue opportunities with basically no one else around. Now *that's* an idea I can get behind. (The idea makes me want to buy a truck right now.)

A well-branded, cool, vintage coffee truck in the parking lot with thousands of runners, a community with a huge running and triathlon community, and no competition? That's doing it differently. And hey, that takes off, you open a downtown location with a great following and we're off to the races. Or back from the races. You get the point.

So ask yourself this objectively: If you are entering a saturated market of breweries, **what are you going to do differently?**

When we opened in Pensacola, there were three downtown breweries: One, McGuire's Irish Pub, was the first craft brewery in Florida, opened in 1987. However, we didn't see it as direct competition because it has largely become an iconic, high-volume restaurant. Pensacola Bay Brewery had been open for about seven years and while mostly distribution, it had a very small taproom off the main stretch of nightlife but still in the historic area. A third brewery, Gulf Coast, had just opened close to downtown, but they invested more in the production side and were not quite walkable from Pensacola's nightlife area.

Because we were entering into a market that hadn't quite seen the national boom of craft breweries, I would often get asked by Pensacolians why we were opening a brewery when there were already breweries in town.

While the easy answer is that a city our size could support more than one or two, we still felt we were offering something different. What made me fall in love with craft beer and this business, just as much as the product, was that feeling you get when you walk into an exceptional taproom. The immersive experience. I loved when the tanks were exposed; it gives a different feeling than seeing them behind a wall. I knew that kind of experience didn't exist yet in our city, and we could create it. My favorite compliment we get is that "your place reminds me of [insert brewery here] in Portland or Denver or Asheville." That's what we were going for, and we invested heavily in that taproom experience to differentiate ourselves.

Reed, our brewing operations director, lived in Asheville before moving down for this project and brought industry-forward knowledge to the table, both front of house and back of house. As my love for craft beer grew, I was traveling all over and experiencing great craft breweries that helped me craft a vision for Perfect Plain.

After losing out on two previous buildings, our third, 50 East Garden Street, was less than a block from the main drag of downtown, giving us by far the best location for foot traffic. We have since become a northern border of the nightlife area, and more development has spawned on our block that was once just filled with architects, attorneys, and engineers, the holy triad of anti-foot traffic.

There was also some room to grow beer-wise in our city. There were no breweries making even kettle sours, for example. To start, we wanted to focus around farmhouse ales – which were also rather rare compared to more standard styles in Pensacola – because we felt it hit that perfect target between approachability for an underserved craft market, the unrelenting heat and suffocating humidity of the Deep South, and the ability to have inspired styles that offered something different than other places.

We felt we were bringing something different. Here is our list of differentiators we identified during our planning phase:

1. We felt we had the best location of any brewery in Pensacola.
2. We felt our taproom space, energy/vibe spoke to our 25-45 target market more than other breweries.
3. We felt we were bringing an experience completely new to our market, both as a brewery or even comparatively as a bar.

4. We felt we could be the first to bring emerging beer styles to our market and do things like bottle releases, a sour program, and an extensive barrel program.
5. We felt that, because of our focus on company culture, hiring, and employee engagement, our customer service could be the best of any bar or brewery in the region (more on tactics for this later).
6. Because of the experience of our leadership team, we would clearly set ourselves apart in branding our company well and utilizing social media well.

Ask yourself what makes you and your idea different. Maybe it's a few things put together like our list.

If you are in the planning or daydreaming phase, write down your list and keep this at the forefront of your decision making. If your brewery is already open, this is still valuable, and should even be more accurate because you've got some measurable achievement to see if these differentiators hold true. If you struggle to identify these, it's a good time to look again at what you should do better than anyone else and how you can pivot priorities to accomplish that goal.

Show it to friends and family who will be honest with you and assess the truth of your vision against the competition in your market. You need honest feedback more than ever. Ask for it.

Before you go any further, notice what I left off my list. I have one rule about establishing your differentiator. **You *cannot* say it's because you'll make the best beer.**

I hope you do. I wish that for you. But there has not been a brewery opened in this nation – all the great ones, and the bad ones, and the mediocre ones – where the belief, and the intent, hasn't been "to make the best beer in town."

Sam Calagione simplifies it further: "You need quality, consistency, and to be well-differentiated."

You can have the nicest equipment in town, and perhaps marketed well it can show the level of quality you strive for. But my lone rule is that the hope of superior beer quality as your sole differentiator is not enough.

Look, no one gets into this business to say they plan on making mediocre beer. But your competition? They said the same thing – they'll make the best beer in town. The three breweries under construction right now in Pensacola? They believe they'll make the best beer in town. The great part about that is the consumer wins. And I believe great breweries create a great beer culture, which takes butts sitting in our pretty white sand at Pensacola Beach – about 85 percent of our tourism primarily comes for the beach – and puts them in our craft beer taprooms further inland.

It's your job to ensure you position your brewery as a unique entity that brings something different to the table.

Write down your list and be honest with yourself. If you can't come up with your differentiator? Start crafting that in your business idea to ensure it always stays front and center. If you are already open and need help crafting that differentiator? Perhaps it's time to focus on one or pivot your business model around something you do that no one else does.

Chapter Homework: Know These Four Things

1. **Write down what will make your brewery different.** How will you change or improve your market while not relying on simply having the best beer?
2. **What is your community's collective beer knowledge?** Think Asheville or Portland on the high end as a benchmark. How many breweries exist in your town? What's the most popular place to get a beer currently?
3. **Know what you know and know what you don't.** If you are a brewer by trade, it's in your best interest to get a very experienced taproom manager to help you with things like customer service, standard operating procedures, point of sale, steps of service for bartenders, and the like. If you are more on the business, marketing, or finance side, make sure you have a sharp mind working for you well in advance of opening who knows their way around building and operating a brewery. Again, don't let ego get in the way of success.
4. **What's a good Saturday night?** No book at a national level will be able to predict an exact market's potential expenses, revenue, or margin. Ask around the area you plan to open your place. More on that shortly.

Chapter 6

Industry Q&A: Dogfish Head CEO Sam Calagione

IN THE CRAFT beer world, he's recognized by first name alone: Sam.

Sam Calagione is the owner of Dogfish Head Craft Brewery in Milton, Delaware, one of the largest and most well-respected independent craft breweries in the world. A pioneer in our industry from the start, he helped push the initial legislation to become Delaware's first brewery. Dogfish Head is a shelf staple in what feels like every single craft beer merchant in the U.S.

Dogfish Head got its start as a brewpub in 1995, well before our recent craft beer boom.

In May 2019 it was announced that Dogfish Head, the thirteenth-largest craft brewery in America according to the BA, would merge with the number two craft beer producer, Boston Beer Company (Sam Adams) in a $300 million deal, bringing two of the most popular and creative craft brewery owners in the world together, Jim Koch and Sam.

The merger will give Boston Beer Company an estimated 2 percent of the market share of all U.S. beer consumption, an astronomical number for a craft beer company against the big beer giants. Dogfish Head is on track to do about 300,000 barrels and $120 million in sales in 2019.

Sam and I sat down in Denver, Colorado in 2019, just before the news of the merger broke, to talk about the state of the industry, his keys to success, and the evolution of the taproom model.

D.C. Reeves: Let's talk about the state of the industry today. You talked about the top jaw and the bottom jaw of craft – the taproom model as one and large-scale distribution on the other. How would you define the industry right now?

Sam Calagione: I say overall, despite what you may read, the love of beer and flavorful, interesting beer is at an all-time high in America. However, I think beer as an industry has to be careful because the data doesn't lie, and more and more drinkers are moving to spirits and wine. And beer consumption with younger drinkers is down.

I think the craft brewing community has to lead on changing that trajectory. Because the world's biggest brewing conglomerates, from my perspective, don't care about the long-term vibrancy of the American beer landscape. They care about harvesting profits out of the American beer landscape. So, it's going to be up to us, the little guys, to keep that excitement alive.

And I would also say I bet we are in a shakeout moment (in 2019) and it's not going to last forever. But I do think we're going to have two, three, four years of stagnant, below-single-digit growth for indie craft. And I think it's an especially challenging moment for breweries of, say, between 20,000 barrels and 200,000 that rely on multi-state distribution for most of their revenue. So I think it's a great thing for you to be doing this book, because I think the strongest economic bet you can make right now is a local tasting room brewery, not a production-oriented brewery with aspirations of going national or regional. It's just the odds are against that today to the degree they weren't when Dogfish was starting out.

DC: Let's talk more about that taproom model and its growth due to the saturation of the market. Do you feel like if you started Dogfish in 2019, that is the way you would go?

SC: Yeah, I would probably have gone with a tasting room model if I was starting today. Essentially, I did. I had a little brewery and a restaurant. Sold everything out my front door for the first two years in 1995.

But with how robust the online beer community is, you don't have to be in a top 20 metro [city] to get a sustainable volume of customers through your front door in a tasting room.

For me, in 1995, trying to figure out how to build a brewery, to find the right bricks and mortar location for my brewery, I thought a good marketing cachet would be the first brewery in a state that hadn't had a brewery since pre-Prohibition, even though I grew up in New England. The closest state by 1995 that still didn't have a brewery was Delaware; that's kind of the reason we ended up there. My wife was from there and the whole state didn't have a brewery yet.

Well, now with 7,500 breweries you can't do that. But I was talking to someone at the Craft Brewers Conference about an interesting similar approach to starting a brewery where they said, "Yeah we researched what town in Massachusetts has the biggest population that doesn't have a brewery yet." And that could be an interesting thing for your readers to aspire to and instead of putting it where you think it should be, look for the most attractive demo, a town that has scale in the right demo and the right legal landscape to allow you to have a tasting room brewery and sell across the bar. Still, some states don't allow that or put a cap on how much beer you can serve. So the triangulating demographic with the best regulatory environment, most entrepreneur-friendly regulatory environment, with a competitive set around you is probably the best driver of where you locate your brewery.

DC: There are two things that I really respect that you guys do at Dogfish. The first is that you talk about the mentality of the market saturating. You've been around well before this swell of interest. You personally could have a bitter feeling about it as if your early innovation is being infringed upon.

SC: I think for any entrepreneur in any industry dominated by massive conglomerates, you have to go into it really focused on the good karma that comes with collaboration instead of the negative energy that comes from focusing on competition. And that has to happen internally – so you know at Dogfish we grew 18 percent two years ago, but now in this environment we're pretty much flat, or up two or three percent.

I can't get mad at my sales team or my marketing team saying we're not hitting our budget. You've got to roll up your sleeves and work together. And that's both an internal philosophy and external.

I did a panel with a brewmaster of Rodenbach. Dogfish is the largest producer of sour beers in America. Rodenbach is the largest producer of sour beers in Europe. We're going to do this collaboration which I'm very excited about.

An instinct might be – well, fuck everyone else, I'm not going to collaborate, I'm going to try to beat them all. I want to be the best sour producer in the world, you know. But we realize right now that we need to work together, to navigate this competitive moment. So, we try to preach that both internally and externally.

DC: The second thing I see that is so awesome about you guys is that thirst for innovation when your company is in a position that it would be much easier not to reinvent or innovate anything. Sometimes it works and sometimes it doesn't, and a "miss" at Dogfish Head would take much longer to overcome. You've got such a huge name in craft, the top of the mountain in U.S. craft, it would be easy to make what you're known for and be done with it.

SC: Well I'd say back to the other question, what does a small brewery have to do in their hometown in order to stay relevant and grow? And you know I said focus more on collaboration than competition.

But I'd say the other thing is that you've got to do three things world class: quality, consistency, and being well-differentiated. And that this both hyper-competitive and hyper-creative moment in our industry, finding that white space and being well-differentiated is a lot harder than it was ten years ago. When we were the only brewery doing breakfast style or fruited sours, it was easy to make that excitement resonate nationally. Now that there's tons of breweries doing those, it's harder to find white space. But it's more rewarding, frankly, when you can still find white space in this competitive moment.

So my recommendation is, I feel like there's too many fast-follower breweries out there. It's like what's not in style today, that's what we're going to brew tomorrow. And I think we as an industry have to be more respectful of other innovations and not step on them. And be more ambitious to find our own innovations instead of relying on what was yesterday's trends to decide what tomorrow should be for us.

Part II
Building Your Microbrewery

IT'S TIME TO do this thing. To build everything from the ground up.

We'll outline some of our experiences and lessons learned, including our financing, and what *you* should be paying attention to in your finances, architecture, permitting, construction, sizing up equipment, and more.

Every construction is unique in size, scope, regulations, and economic climate. But we hope that our story can spark the right questions to ask your local vendors and officials.

One right question from this section could save you thousands and thousands of dollars. It's time to start building.

Chapter 7

Tips to Start Your Business Plan

I WAS THE guy walking into banks with no previous business or entrepreneurial experience. No craft beer experience (other than drinking a bunch of it – at least *some* bankers found that funny). Having a sound, meticulous 41-page business plan with financials that added up, were realistic, and showed a profit was my only weapon. And probably some luck.

Once I knew I would be able to qualify for the Small Business Administration portion of my loan, I pounded the pavement for banks that would take the rest of the loan. We probably reached out to about 15 banks and got about three serious inquiries, ultimately deciding between two banks in the end.

The lesson I learned is that banks are much more subjective than you would think. I had this illusion that all banks plugged your numbers into the same formula, and they'd all have the same answer. They are way more subjective than that. They may have a larger or smaller pool of dollars earmarked for commercial loans than other banks, so the timing can be wrong or right. Banks that have done a brewery deal before may be more apt to take on another one if they had success with the previous experience – or less apt to do it if it flopped.

Know there's a lot of subjectivity with lenders, and that just illuminates the crucial nature of a sound business plan.

Then I remembered I had never done one before.

Where to begin?

Looking for an aid to get this crucial business plan done, in 2016 I found Liveplan.com, an online service that helps you format and build your business plan. They don't do the research or the work for you, but the software really helps with building out the financial projections and guides you with some strategy on how to write each particular section of the business plan.

It was a nominal cost to ensure that the plan was done right, and I can't imagine how much time I saved compared to doing it from scratch in a Microsoft Word document.

Quick Business Plan Checklist

1. Executive summary: A short, easily digestible version of your business plan.
   o What problem are you solving in the market?
   o What's your solution, in a nutshell?
   o What does your market look like?
   o Who are your competitors?
2. Quick financial projection.

You'll go into more detail on each of those later in the plan. When you're thinking about what to include, think about the bank president who may be interested but will be relying on the loan officer to dig through all those extra pages.

I won't go line by line, but here are some other key things to be sure you cover in the full business plan:

- Deep detail on competition, target market, the problem and solution.
- Company overview and key team members, mentors, and investors. Lenders and investors like to see who is in your corner.
- Your plan for how the company will operate day to day, how you will market your company, and what the key metrics of success will be.
- Profile of all of your competition in the market – *this is where it's time to brag about what's going to make you different.*
- Financial forecast: Three years of projected financials, including month-by-month financials for the first year. This is pretty much a guess, of course – I showed us distributing 250 barrels in our first year when we didn't do a drop in our first 18 months. But give it your best shot. Be sure you aren't just providing graphs, but

also an explanation of what those graphs are showing. Remember, bankers aren't going to know what the intricacies of distribution look like.

■ Include your projected Profit and Loss Statement, Balance Sheet, and Cash Flow Statement.

For a startup company, a sound business plan is paramount. You need it for investors, you need it for banks, you need it for your own sanity. One day when you're a billionaire, you may not need one. But today, plan on investing time into creating a sound plan.

Chapter 8
Figuring Out Your Financials

ONE OF THE most overwhelming parts of opening a craft brewery is trying to figure out the numbers. It doesn't really matter if you are a brewer or have a background in finance; when a new, unproven business enters a market, there are so many variables that can affect the success of the brewery that no level of financial expertise can predict with confidence if your business model will be successful.

In other words, if you feel like that whatever you're going to put down for projected revenue, expenses, payroll, utilities, taxes, insurance, and more is just a guess, don't worry. We've all been there. It *is* a guess. The goal should be to make that guess as educated as possible.

I was always intentionally conservative on revenue and very liberal on expenses. I wanted to make sure that we would still be successful even if we had more expenses and less revenue than I hoped. It's important not to daydream here. This is the reality of the feasibility of your business and all the hard work you plan on putting in in the years to come. There's no room for lying to ourselves.

Later in the book I share my talk with Audra Gaiziunas, a brewery finance consultant and CEO of Bhramari Brewing Co. in Asheville, North Carolina, to get her expert perspective on what she has seen from startup and young breweries and what they should be paying attention to most.

Before we get there, here are some questions and concerns you should be considering as you project your numbers.

Understanding Top-Line Revenue

Top-line revenue projection means an estimate of every sales dollar that comes into the building.

Every brewery should have as firm an understanding as possible of what it can realistically make in its first year of operations. This includes beer sales, merchandise, event space fees/rentals, wine, soda, liquor, other beverages, and any other avenues you have to create revenue.

If your brewery is already open, you should have a projected line item budget based off the previous year's revenues with adjustments based on what's to come in the new year.

This is the most vital statistic you should research during the exploratory phase of your potential brewery. It should be well researched. Here are the questions we sought answers to before we opened, and these are questions that any brewer should know as a new brewery or a brewery-in-planning. Expenses can be controlled much easier than revenue. If your idea is bad, your beer is bad and/or your location is bad, you can't magically double your revenue. So this understanding is paramount.

Understanding Cost of Goods Sold

While it will be much more difficult to accurately project all of your overhead expenses until you are in business, you should be able to get a firm grasp of the items that make up the costs to produce each pint or batch of beer. Those include:

- Grain
- Hop
- Fruit/fermentables
- Yeast (Repitching yeast can make this harder to track.)
- Gas/electric (This one can be tough when everything is on one bill; it will be a guestimate that your brewhouse manufacturer can perhaps assist with. At Perfect Plain only natural gas is used on the brew

side, so I dedicate that entire bill to Cost of Goods Sold(COGS) and guesstimate a little electric expense for glycol chiller, etc.)

- Pertinent brewing software like Ekos (Note that an accountant may take this one out.)
- Direct labor (This includes labor cost attributed *only* to the production of beer, such as brewers who do nothing other than work on the brew side. If you pay them a salary and they also bartend two nights a week, for example, that makes the calculation more difficult.)

Once you have these numbers, you can drill them down to a per-batch cost, and even a per-pint cost. This can help you determine what your taproom beer price needs to be.

So, let's start trying to apply accuracy to your projections.

How Much Beer Can I Sell in My Taproom?

Everything you project about your business will be constructed around this number, so it's important to get as educated a guess as you can and use this projected number of barrels sold uniformly throughout your business plan. Don't project that you will sell 1,000 barrels in the taproom in Year 1, then not have your expenses – think Cost of Goods Sold, labor to produce that amount, and so on – match what it takes to create 1,000 barrels. Whatever you decide this number to be, keep it consistent throughout your business plan. That shows lenders that you are competent with your plan, and it will ensure that your business has the chance to be successful. Inconsistencies in any fashion cause concern.

It is your obligation as a business owner to do your best to understand your market. To truly do so, you need to understand what a *realistic* top-line revenue goal is. Many prospective breweries may just guess what they think or hope they will sell out of the taproom in a year, guess how much they will distribute, and put a rough number on it. I think that's irresponsible, mainly because with a little bit of legwork you can turn a blind guess into a fairly educated one.

No business, regardless of industry, should ever open without knowing what the market is ready for.

If you are building a brewery in Chicago or New York, great! Plenty of market. And plenty of rent payment. Plenty of labor cost, too.

We can all think of a brewery we know that makes great beer but didn't invest in their location. We can all think of a brewery that jumped right to distribution without building its brand and is struggling. Is there bad luck in business? Of course. But many of these issues are manmade. It's about doing your homework and getting an unbiased account of what the market can realistically bear.

Calculating Top-Line Revenue

Is there a calculation for easily projecting top-line revenue? By the square foot? By taproom seats? I'm not a believer that there's a hard and fast calculation for revenue. There are just too many moving parts. Outside of numbers of seats and your taproom space, there is your market. Your location. Your average price per beer based on your market.

You can Google and read and ask folks to help you project on the ProBrewer.com message boards until your heart is content looking for this silver bullet formula. Trust me, we did the same thing. It would be nice if there were an accurate equation, like selling X barrels per seat per year. I've seen people take stabs at that before, but they're just not accurate for every situation.

Think about it: If I just went into our taproom tomorrow and threw 40 more seats in there, other than crowding all of my customers, would my revenue go up exponentially by that amount? If I added 200 square feet to my taproom, but all I did was put a shuffleboard table there, it would immediately lower my sales per square foot.

I like to look at revenue projections as a whole. I think we can sell X beers/ciders/cocktails per night, or per week.

If you don't have a friend in the business, the best advice I can give you to get a solid estimate is just to go to a bar you feel has a good reputation closest to your future (or desired) location and ask, *What's a good Friday night in sales? What's a good Saturday night in sales? What's a good Monday in sales?* Often, even the bartenders know this answer because they print off the sales report each night before closing. If you aren't going to serve food – we use food trucks at Perfect Plain and are on our way to buying our own – make sure that is not included.

Well that's a bar, not a brewery! When you're estimating taproom sales – not distribution revenues – you are in essence a bar with a better vibe and a cooler story about your product in the fact that it's made on site. Welcome to the advantage of the brewery taproom. (Side diatribe: This same advantage is starting to be created in the high-end craft cocktail world, handcrafted with care and with a great bar environment; although the liquor isn't manufactured on site in the vast majority of cases, it speaks to the customer in the same way.)

One thing we all love about the brewing industry is its collaborative nature. What you'll find is that entrepreneurs in general are exactly the same. So, reach out to a bar owner, buy that person a coffee, and pick his or her brain.

While you're working through a business plan, I can help you with some of our metrics. We do about 55 percent of our overall business on Friday and Saturday night, and a little over 70 percent of our combined sales Thursday through Sunday.

What Do I Need These Projections for?

First, your sanity. It's going to take a lot mentally and financially for you, your family, and your investors for you to pull this project off. Shouldn't you feel certain that if done as planned, you are going to be successful?

A Business Plan So Banks Can Loan You Money   Three years of sales projections are the norm, and banks like to see projections for three years. But the further and further you get from Day 1, the less likely the situation at your brewery is even in the stratosphere of what you expected. So, don't rack your brain trying to come up with your exact top-line revenue in Month 29. Be meticulous about understanding your first year of revenue, then in Year 2 or Year 3 you can add a flat growth percentage unless you are predicting a major change in revenue based on a particular event (i.e. you are proposing to a bank or investors that you are opening a second location, a production facility, etc. If you say that in your business plan, make *sure* that's reflected in your numbers; why would a bank loan money to someone who says it will invest in something that returns nothing in revenue?).

We all understand that business plans are educated guesses. Things happen. They change. Weather being too hot or too cold can affect your business.

Key Considerations for Any Top-Line Revenue Projection

Spillage/Product Dumping

Even if you have the most talented brewery staff, elite draft equipment, and the most steady-handed bartenders that walk our beautiful earth, you will not be getting exactly 124 draft pints out of each keg. Projecting as such is an immediate recipe to miss your projections.

We factored in spillage of 11 percent. I got that number from a close friend of mine, Scott Zepp, cofounder of World of Beer. This doesn't always mean spilling in a literal sense. Fellow brewers may come in with whom you want to exchange beer, right? You think you may allow your staff to have a free beer after their shift? Think a keg may get over-carbonated and pour straight foam for a frustrating amount of time? Think someone will complain about a beer and want to exchange it?

Unless you hire the perfect brewers, think you won't be dumping a batch of beer that doesn't meet your standards. Doug Reiser of Burial Beer Co. told me he's considered requiring that a minimum number of batches be expected to go down the drain each year. That should tell us something about expecting to put your name only on quality product, but also that you shouldn't expect every single beer to be countable.

All of these things will happen.

Let's say you project you will sell your beers at $5 per pint multiplied by 248 pints in a barrel (two half-barrel kegs), which equals $1,240 of top-line revenue. Now back out 11 percent of that. Your true top line is $1,103 per barrel. A taproom-only model will be even higher than 11 percent, we've learned. One week of foaming issues on the taps, for example, can eat quite a bit of beer.

If you project that you will move 400 barrels in your taproom in a year, without spillage, that would be projected as $496,000 of top-line revenue. With spillage, that total sinks to $441,440. You're talking about a significant difference of more than $55,000. You can see where leaving this out can be impactful.

Consistency   If you say you are going to sell 600 barrels of beer in your taproom, and you are going to show that as revenue, make sure your Cost of Goods Sold (your costs of materials, utilities, etc., to make the beer itself) reflects the expenses required to make those barrels. Often I've seen business plans where someone bumped up their revenue projections but forgot to bump up the expenses. While that may look nice on a profit and loss statement, a lender or potential investor may be asking about your astronomical gross margin. And that's the moment you realize that you changed revenue and not expenses, and that's not the setting in which you want to discover that mistake.

I know crunching numbers isn't fun, but it's necessary, and a responsibility to yourself, to your family, and to any potential investors who will be on this journey with you.

Average Beer Price   You can crunch numbers, figure out the margin you need, and price it accordingly. I actually tend to work backward on this one. I like to see what the **successful** breweries and craft beer bars that align with your product, atmosphere, and experience are charging, then run the numbers and see if that beer price works in my financials.

We charge between $5.50 and $7 per 12-ounce pour, depending on style, and will increase that price once the beers from our barrel program are ready. While that made us the most expensive brewery in town by a slight margin, we also do more experimentation with more expensive ingredients than other breweries in our area. In addition, we compared our costs to other craft beer bars with similar prime locations. We figured if they were successful in charging *more* than us for craft beer that wasn't made on site, if our quality was there, we should have no issue getting this price point on quality beer that was made inhouse. Not exactly scientific, but perhaps a more commonsense approach to setting your beer pricing.

Don't be influenced by what your friend's brewery charges across the country. That has no bearing on what your beer price can and should be.

Pricing Merchandise and Wine or Cocktails   Again, this is rather subjective based on market. But this is when your brand matters – we'll talk more on that later in the book. But merchandise, when executed correctly, can be a significant portion of your business and a great way to build your exposure. It amounted to about 5 percent of our top-line sales in 2018. While that doesn't seem like a lot, think about how much more that is than a standard bar would be.

So while quality product should be your primary focus, merchandise can be enough of boost that it's worth curating some quality options. Don't treat it as an afterthought. Not only will subpar merch hurt sales, but if poorly done it sends the message that you don't care if people wear it.

I tend to actually take less of a profit on merchandise than most breweries to ensure top-quality products. Why? Think about all those crappy, uncomfortable 5K run and festival T-shirts you never wear again. A top-end quality shirt, hat, or the like sends your customers the message that you care about having nice merchandise – a reflection that you must care about your beer too. And guess what? If that shirt doesn't shrink to half its size after one wash, they may wear it more than once! That's free advertising for you.

On the "other drinks" side, before we added a liquor license to be able to serve spirits, we stayed pretty tight to about 12 percent of our overall revenue in wine sales. That said, we were also close to downtown near many restaurants, so I'd venture to guess we were likely pretty high on the scale nationally. Since adding liquor, our sales of wine have dropped but liquor has surged to about 15–17 percent of our sales. As I maintain, this will vary wildly market to market, based on location, average income, and the level of consumer craft beer knowledge in your area.

Top-Line Expenses   Much like revenue, projecting expenses – while slightly more predictable – is still truly a guess. But as someone investing every cent to their name, this was the one I was most worried about. I made it my mission to ensure I would not miss a significant expense.

Here is a working early draft of our prediction on top-line revenue and itemized expenses. Use this as a template only – this was months before we opened, and I wouldn't count on these numbers being exact for anyone. However, take the time to make your best guess at these categories.

Projected Profit & Loss

	FY2018	FY2019	FY2020
Revenue	$519,990	$680,136	$696,736
Direct Costs	$118,854	$144,982	$148,994
Gross Margin	$401,136	$535,154	$547,742
Gross Margin %	77%	79%	79%
Operating Expenses			
Salary	$90,500	$92,400	$94,395
Employee-Related Expenses	$10,600	$10,980	$11,379
POS	$1,548	$1,548	$1,548
Advertising	$10,400	$13,603	$13,934
Credit Card Fees	$10,400	$13,603	$13,934
Insurance	$10,000	$10,000	$10,000
Utilities (brew incl. in COGS)	$24,000	$24,000	$24,000
Accounting Fees	$3,600	$3,600	$3,600
Assorted Barroom Materials	$600	$600	$600
Brewery equipment	$2,400	$2,400	$2,400
Brewery Entertainment	$12,000	$12,000	$12,000
Property Tax	$5,000	$5,000	$5,000
Misc. Bills (garbage, Wi-Fi, license music fees, cable, etc.)	$9,000	$9,000	$9,000
Canning / Keg Materials	$15,000	$30,000	$30,000
Total Operating Expenses	$205,048	$228,733	$231,791
Operating Income	$196,088	$306,421	$315,951
Interest Incurred	$62,278	$59,661	$56,901
Depreciation and Amortization	$20,000	$20,000	$20,000
Income Taxes	$0	$0	$0
Total Expenses	$406,180	$453,377	$457,687
Net Profit	$113,810	$226,759	$239,049
Net Profit / Sales	22%	33%	34%

Make sure you invest time in finding out what your "break even" number is. If the lease payment is too high or payroll is too heavy, this is the way you will be able to find out.

Projections Homework

1. Do you know what your projected top-line revenue is? Can you explain and back up why you chose that number?
2. Do you know what your projected top-line expenses are?

Chapter 9

Finance Q&A with Bhramari Brewing CEO Audra Gaiziunas

AUDRA GAIZIUNAS[1] STARTED a company called Brewed for Her Ledger, an accounting, management, and consultancy firm that combines her financial expertise with her passion for craft beer.

She spent time as Dogfish Head's controller in 2009–10, Mother Earth Brewing Company's CFO in 2011–14, and then took over as CEO at Bhramari Brewing Co. in downtown Asheville in 2016, navigating a miracle turnaround from what seemed to be inevitable closure to a thriving brewery in the heart of one of the nation's most competitive craft beer environments.

She has worked with more than 100 breweries in all phases of life to help them start, grow, and prosper.

While I can speak to some of our financial projections, targets, and how we modeled those numbers at Perfect Plain, Audra brings immense data and perspective of best (and worst) practices in our craft industry. And in an ever-saturating market, understanding the numbers can be the difference between success and failure.

She discusses the most common missteps, how to prepare financially, and the key metrics you should be following in your brewery business.

D.C. Reeves: When you work with a taproom-focused brewery, be it a startup or an existing one, what is the most common thing you see happening with its finances?

---

[1] Bhramari Brewing Co. (https://www.bhramaribrewing.com/) and Brewed For Her Ledger (https://www.brewedforherledger.com/).

Audra Gaiziunias: From a financial perspective, the number one issue that we face is opening and operating undercapitalized. Make sure that you have enough working capital on hand from the very get go. That really stems from a larger issue of planning, and spending enough time planning, throughout the entire build-out – what the taproom is going to look like, what your brew system looks like. A lot of people have invested quite a bit.

They'll budget quite a bit for their equipment, but they forget about something like the process piping, which is going to be largely dependent upon your layout of your entire facility. They get the quote for all their equipment, for example, and they forget all the process piping and that it can be up to a third of your total equipment costs in addition. Make sure that you have that aside and you understand the layout when you ask for your quote. Come back for a second one just to get on process piping once you've got your schematic design.

In many cases, the brewery asks for too little. It results in asking for too small a loan, and then they end up eating into their working capital because they hadn't budgeted for item X or item Y because they hadn't put enough time into planning their entire layout and what the brewhouse should look like.

Then when it comes time to open, they're short on working capital because they hadn't budgeted enough for that. Once they're open on the working capital side, the key is having three months of expectant cash outflows on hand or at least access to that because you never know. You're going to be so gloriously inefficient in those first six months of operations. It doesn't matter that you have it going through a distributor. You'll have some years that are not up to snuff. As you're trying to dial in your carbonation, you're trying to dial in all these other factors and getting everything just right, you're still burning through quite a bit of cash.

I run into this situation pretty often that breweries open, and they're running out of cash or they stifle themselves from that perspective that they can't reinvest it back to growth. They're just trying to scrape together any penny they can to put a grain order together just to brew enough beer. To see these situations occur with shortages of beer . . . these breweries are opening their taprooms and they've run out of beer within the first two days of opening. Now they have to put guest taps on. A lot of that comes not just from poor planning of brewing, it's really more of a working capital issue. I see that they haven't brewed enough beer, but that could be largely dependent upon you not having set aside enough cash for the inventory to brew the beer to keep up with the demand.

That's the biggest thing that I see – not putting enough money together, not planning enough, not asking for a large enough loan, and not having enough working capital set aside for your day of open.

DC: Let's say I just read your answer and I'm opening a place. Now my eyes are wide open. Can you define planning? Obviously, everybody's situation is different in different markets, sizes, etc. But from a general sense, you say without proper planning, what do you look at as an expert as planning properly?

AG: Yes, planning. That's a good question. It is putting together a sources-and-uses statement. The uses section of that statement is, line by line, all the equipment, all the build-out costs: HVAC, plumbing, design build-out. If you're building from the ground up, what materials you are using, what your general contractor has given you in terms of a quote, etc. Then going through the entire brew house: the boiler, the grain handling system, pots, small things like that. It's really understanding the entire process flow and following the process flow through and making sure that you have line items for the budget for your sources-and-uses statement from Day 1 and know that it's valuable and that you can change it.

That's fine, and then you move on to the taproom or the draft system. What does that look like? The taproom layout, what does that look like? What does that entail? Are you going to be investing in landscaping? Some places require fencing, and that could be easily $10,000 by itself.

Understanding your parcel that you're working with, the property that you're working with, and really working hand in hand with your architects and your engineers on the entire design to understand all the cost implications that are going into it, so not just fully depending on your architect to give you a drawing. Understand what that drawing means and how that could create some implications in terms of cost for you that you should build out into your budget. Having a very thorough sources-and-uses statement will basically define what you'll be left with on Day 1 for a working capital.

Then there are the startup expenses. Say you have a six-month build-out time period. All the costs that you're going to incur, all of your cash flows that you're going to incur in that six-month time period's growth build-out, so that you still have, on day of open, those three months of expected cash outflows on hand.

DC: You bring such great perspective because you work with different breweries of all sizes that have different sources of revenue, be it distribution, be it a taproom, or even other things outside of that. From a financial perspective, what do you see as the advantages of starting as a taproom-focused model?

AG: Purely from a finance standpoint, thinking of profit margin, you should not be making any less than 85 percent gross margin in your taproom, and even that is if you are using something expensive like agave all the time for your materials. That does not include all of your direct labor. That is just your materials. You should be shooting for 85 percent or higher. Most of my taproom clients, taproom focus clients, are operating in the 92 percent gross margin range. From that point, we take away your front-of-house labor and your taproom (overhead), because there's so many aspects. Some of those are split between the brewhouse and production and the taproom, so you have to work out and delineate what your production versus staff reduction labor is to figure what your true gross margin is when you have direct labor involved versus part of overhead. That will be in your SG&A (selling, general, and administrative expenses form), regardless. Most of mine average about 92 percent gross margin on materials only. You should not be lower than 85. That's only if you're using honey and agave, for example, as your primary fermentables.

DC: Compare that to the distribution model. Not even counting the practical challenges of selling it, getting it out there, sales people, all that stuff. Again, purely financial, how does that compare to somebody who might be more distribution focused?

AG: Someone who is more distribution focused is going to be about 52 percent to 65 percent gross margin because they do not have that price realization that you have in the taproom. In the taproom, you have 100 percent price realization. You don't have to give any of that up to a wholesaler. Taproom model is the easiest way to prove your concepts, but it is also the least amount of risk financially to take. You're going to gain your investment back. Your payback period is going to be shortest that way, but it also involves the least amount of risk. If you need to get more cash to the drawer, bring more people to the taproom. That's what I always tell people if they have started out with more of a distribution model and haven't focused so much on their taproom. You can do it with taproom-only releases, bottles, cans, whatever they may be. Bring in that cash flow. That takes care of a lot of the situation.

The taproom model is just a reduction of risk. The greatest profit margin brings in the greatest amount of cash in the door. Not necessarily in total dollars, but as a percentage of sales, and it allows you to break even most quickly.

DC: Okay, so let's say somebody's in the next stage. They've been doing this a couple of years. What do you see as the green light of saying hey, you're ready to add distribution to your established taproom model? When do you look at the books and say maybe it is time to look at driving in a higher dollar volume at a lower margin? What would you want to see from them before they make that leap?

AG: They would need to explain distribution to me where it makes more sense. Hopefully, it's not from a panic-stricken perspective of where you realize you have to expand your footprint just to be sustainable so you're doing it just to get dollars in the door. I have seen breweries do that before. Not advised.

There are different motivations that people have. Ideally what I like to see is that you can cover all of your cash outflows. You don't really have a place that you want to expand more than the taproom side of things, and so now you have an excess amount of cash flow that you're putting into a savings account, to be used to put equity injection down for either a loan, or you can invest in it yourself, in the expansion of the taproom or in the expansion of the operation.

Also, your investors have to be on board with you investing it back in the brewery rather than in the form of distributions to them. Part of that conversation really stems from who your investment team is and who has provided the paid-in capital from the get-go. You may be ready for distribution, but they want to have some distributions themselves before you sign on with a wholesaler and move on. Ideally it's when you already met all of your cash outflow obligations and, if you even have any debt left anymore, but a very strong debt service coverage and you have agreement with your wholesalers to move forward because you've then proven your concepts both financially as well as brand-wise if you use wholesalers that are interested at looking at you.

DC: Our Director of Brewing Operations, Reed Odeneal, has written a chapter on right-sizing your brewing system and our experience at Perfect Plain. But what advice do you give when it comes to sizing equipment for the brewery and what should people be looking out for?

AG: As you start, a lot of it has to do with the population density in the area. If you're a taproom-focused model that really is not going to be focused on outside distribution and you're really wanting to bring people to taproom, I usually start with a 10-barrel or a smaller system. If you have distribution in mind eventually, then I'd start with a 15-barrel and a one- to two-barrel pilot system, but usually a two or three. If you can afford a three-barrel pilot, add that on as well because then you'll be set with both the experimentals and you can continue to stay nimble as you brew new beers and can change things out, but then you're ready for distribution with a 15-barrel that you have set aside. You're prepared for both sides.

If it's taproom only, 10-barrel. It's the least amount of risk that you have, and it still allows you to be nimble enough to switch things out and not clam up your entire space with too much of the same brand of beer.

DC: A two-part question: First, what are those two or three pieces of advice you like to share with pre-opening and young breweries, and what are maybe the two or three metrics that you like to track if you are a brewery owner or manager?

AG: Okay, young brewery. Understand truly what your cost of goods is comprised of. That really stems from designing your chart of accounts to be aligned with your business model. Understand what your business model is, your different revenue streams that you have, your varying cost streams that you have, and make sure you design your chart of accounts accordingly to match up with those revenue streams. Otherwise, you're going to be pulling data from every which way, trying to do work-around solutions and trying to figure out if they're moving in their right direction via Excel. Do you have systems in place that should do the work for you? They only work for you if you design them correctly in the first place. Take the time to design your chart of accounts, because I think that's super important even if you know nothing about finance. If you don't know how to do that, find somebody with a brewery background who will do that for you. It should not take a great amount of time. It'll save you so much heartache down the road.

Second, if you don't understand how your financials work, what they look like, what they should look like, you should pay somebody with some financial knowledge to look at them for you, or have somebody on your advisory board who could help you out just in understanding your financials. Another choice is to get some basic financial knowledge through your local community college if you don't have some. If you have anybody with a finance or accounting background at your brewery, there are so many free courses that are usually involved through your community college, through the Small Business Administration, and other organizations. There are economic development corporations. They put out a lot of these basic financial classes so that you can get yourself well-versed. Those are the two big things.

As far as financial metrics go, understand your margins. Understand what a gross margin is and understand what your weighted average cost of goods looks like based on all the styles that you have offered. Make sure to separate that out between your taproom and then wholesale. Yeah, that's big. Then understanding your prime costs is another one. Prime costs are your costs of your raw materials of all your direct materials and direct labor added together, because what's left over for overhead is really what you need to be able to operate the brewery. If all of those are fixed costs versus variable costs, you may be running yourself short and ragged. Understand your prime costs and understand what your gross margin are. Those are the two big ones. The overall dollar sales are not as important as they are as terms of margins. Margins are much more important than top-line sales at the end of the end if you're building a model that's sustainable for you and for what you're trying to accomplish.

Having $1 million in sales in the first year can be phenomenal for one taproom, and it could be not enough for another one based on what their model looks like. The key is more in margin rather than top-line.

Then cash flow. Cash, cash, cash, cash, cash, cash is everything. Make sure that you have at least three months' worth of cash on hand, and if you don't, access to those three months' worth of cash on hand via line of credit. You have to have a piggy bank to reach into if needed.

DC: So how about all the way to the bottom line? What do you like to see at a taproom-focused model? Are you wanting that 25 percent or 26 percent? What do you want to see all the way to the bottom line, that net income?

AG: Well, it depends on whether you're involving food or not. A restaurant in general is not very profitable, and you have a lot of waste. There's a lot that goes into a restaurant. If you're serving food, it's more acceptable to have a lower net income, but most of my breweries that I work with, they range in net income from about 9 percent to about 15 percent. If you're only serving beer, it's possible to do higher than that. If you have food, you can expect 9 percent to 15 percent and still be sustainable and still have enough that you roll into retained earnings to reinvest back into the brewery.

If you don't, there's no limit really. It depends on what your business model looks like, but you want to make at least that. If you're making that with food, you will make more without food, but you won't keep the people there as long.

Based on about 140 different breweries and data points I've collected, we know that a guest ticket averages 0.7 pints less if you do not have food.

Chapter 10

Finding the Dollars to Get Started

You wouldn't start making beer without a recipe. So why would you attempt to start a business without understanding where your capital is going to come from? This chapter discusses some of the ins and outs of getting your first business loan. It's not as impossible as you think.

An overarching theme in this book is that we felt it important to prepare as much as possible to eliminate the unexpected. Our building took four months longer to close than we hoped, for example. We were going to open in July, then August, then September, then October. We actually opened November 21, 2017.

In this chapter we'll focus on understanding your road map for getting the money you need to start your brewery. There are three ways to go about the search for money:

1. Private/equity financing
2. Private loan (friends and family, etc.)
3. Bank/Small Business Administration financing

The most fun one, which I know nothing about, would be to be independently wealthy and pay cash for everything. Wouldn't that be nice.

Equity financing – taking in investment in exchange for equity in the company – is a common practice.

Private loans without exchanging equity are not unheard of in this industry – asking family members or friends for a loan being the most likely source – but probably less so than other industries because of the capital-intense start.

The most common method is raising enough funds between ownership and investors, then bringing in bank and potentially Small
Business Administration (SBA) financing.

I sold off 30 percent of Perfect Plain to help raise the owner equity
needed to engage in what was called the SBA 504 Loan Program.

Of course, these programs, terms, and procedures can change, and there
could be specific lending rules in your state that differ from our experience
in Florida. The best thing you can do is to ask around about who completes
the most SBA commercial loans in your area and pick that person's brain.

Getting a loan from the government hasn't excited you yet? (Ha.)
Let me explain the real value of this program. The SBA, on your
behalf, ultimately positions you as a significantly more attractive borrower with local banks. The pie chart shows the breakdown.

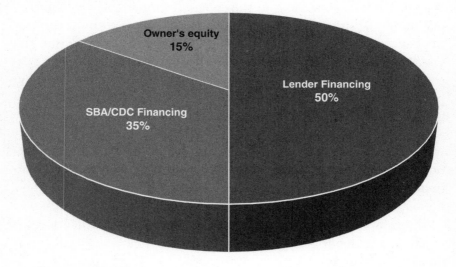

If you're approved for this program, the financing breaks down this
way. The borrower, as a startup, puts up 15 percent of the cost of the
project (owner's equity drops to 10 percent on a refinance or a second
project). To keep math simple, let's say the project cost is $1 million.
That means you will need to come up with $150,000 in cash.

Initially, the local bank that agrees to partner with the SBA comes
up with the other 85 percent of the loan. However, once your build-
out is completed, the SBA comes in and takes 35 percent of the project ($350,000 in this example), while the local institution hangs on
to 50 percent ($500,000). There's your $1 million.

Here's the kicker that makes this all work. The reason you are more attractive to a bank in this program is because the SBA is willing to take a "second position" on the note, meaning if you were to default on your loan, the local bank would have the chance to recoup its $500,000 completely before the SBA would be able to come in and recoup its money.

The SBA becomes the bank's safety net, allowing it to have only a $500,000 loan resting against $1 million in assets, significantly raising the likelihood that the local bank can be made whole in case of a default.

This SBA 504 Loan required that we purchase property, and Perfect Plain bought its building. The SBA also had a 7A loan program that was more in line with someone looking to lease. The terms and stipulations were different, but the common denominator in any SBA loan is that it positions you as a borrower much better with a bank than hoping to go the conventional route. (By the way, considering the uniqueness of a brewery build-out and the expense you would be putting in someone else's building, I unequivocally recommend that you purchase your building, or at a minimum, get a lease with an option to purchase later.)

And hey, if you can get a conventional bank to loan you 85 percent of the money without involving the SBA, then congratulations. You not only have fantastic credit, but you're wealthy, or have immense small business experience, or you or your parents are mortgaging their houses against the loan at a minimum.

Translation: The litmus test to borrow at a conventional level is much, much higher. So if you are not already a renowned local entrepreneur, or don't have very wealthy partners willing to guarantee the loan personally, then I'd start at SBA.gov.

Bear in mind, this financing often cannot include working capital – the startup dollars you need to buy inventory, pay your first couple of payrolls, and so on. It also does not pay for anything intangible like branding costs.

So I would, at a minimum, add 60 days of your projected expenses as a line item of funds to raise. Working capital, because of the inability to leverage it against any assets that a bank or an individual cannot recoup in the case of nonpayment – that Perfect Plain logo isn't worth a whole lot if the business is bankrupt – are the hardest dollars

What Is the 504 Loan Program?

The SBA 504 Loan Program is a powerful economic development loan program that offers small businesses another avenue for business financing, while promoting business growth and job creation. As of February 15, 2012, the $50 billion in 504 Loans has created over 2 million jobs. This program is a proven success and win-win-win for the small business, the community, and participating lenders.

The 504 Loan Program provides approved small businesses with long-term, fixed-rate financing used to acquire fixed assets for expansion or modernization. 504 Loans are made available through Certified Development Companies (CDCs), SBA's community-based partners for providing 504 Loans.

Am I Eligible?
In addition to operating your business for profit, you'll need to have a feasible business plan and relevant management expertise to be considered eligible for a 504 Loan. As with any business seeking SBA's financial assistance, you're also required to do business in the United States or its territories. And you must have tried to use other financial resources, including personal assets, before applying for a loan. Here are some other requirements to consider:

- Your business must have a tangible net worth of less than $15 million.
- Your business must have an average net income of less than $5 million after taxes for the preceding two years.
- You must have the ability to repay the loan on time from the projected operating cash flow of your business.

How Can I Use the Funds?
Loan funds can be used to:

- Purchase land
- Purchase existing buildings
- Purchase long-term machinery and equipment
- Purchase improvements (including grading, street improvements, utilities, parking lots, and landscaping)

- Build new facilities or modernize, renovate, or convert existing facilities

A 504 Loan cannot be used for:

- Working capital or inventory
- Consolidating, repaying, or refinancing debt (although for a portion of the project, you may refinance debt associated with buying or renovating equipment or facilities)
- Speculation or investment in rental real estate

Source: Small Business Administration

to borrow. So if you have that friend or family member who has the means to support you as you pull together dollars for a project, keep this in mind. The person who has the most faith in you may be willing to help finance an unsecured, working capital loan with interest-only payments for the introductory 12 or 18 months as you get the business off the ground.

Key Questions on Financing

How do I come up with the owner's equity?

In short, you've got to have it on hand, borrow it from a wonderful family member or friend, or sell a percentage of your company, also known as equity.

The obvious threshold is that owning 51 percent of the company means you are the controlling interest. I'm going to grossly oversimplify this (an attorney, your potential lender, and/or an accountant can help with this), but also keep in mind that there are additional responsibilities, whether that means requirements to be on loan guarantees, licensing, or other considerations, at selling 10 percent in some cases, and certainly at 20 percent. For example, the SBA requires that anyone with 20 percent ownership or more must sign on to its portion of the loan. Any lender you deal with will have their own set of requirements.

And remember, equity is for life. You don't get that back. In the case of Perfect Plain, I knew that to be the primary investor, the guarantor of the loans, and the common thread among all investors, I wanted to have controlling interest given the risk in play to execute this project.

So I'm willing to sell equity to raise capital. How do I decide what a startup company is worth?

This is one of life's great mysteries. You can find so many different theories on how to calculate this, but for a pre-revenue company, and especially as a first-time business owner, nailing a number is like shooting blind.

At Perfect Plain, I made the valuation on the company very reasonable for the other investors because I was also much more concerned about picking strategic partners than I was just to get every dollar possible. So I believe the deal was more than fair for those investors, but they brought something to us as well. All three of our investors brought industry knowledge, business operations knowledge, or potential loan capital to the table. Perhaps more important, all three were not looking for a "quick buck" on their investment. I was sure that philosophically we were aligned in the fact that we could roll potential profits into growing the business.

My best advice is to consult with someone you know who has opened a brewery or a bar in your home market with similar circumstances (startup expenses, potential revenue similarities, etc.) and see how they came up with their company valuation. Setting a valuation is yet another reason that investing time and sweat into a sound business plan creates value for an owner. Putting your best foot forward to investors means you are much more likely to succeed.

Chapter Homework

1. **How much money will your project take to complete?** As the old saying goes, and for good reason, expect it to cost twice as much and to take twice as long. Be sure that you don't fall victim to undercapitalization. Overestimate your build-out expenses. Overestimate your equipment expenses. I know it's tempting to lower those numbers so it "lowers" the cash you need to get your place open, but it's just a mirage. Instead, you'll need money when you

least expect it, or you will make unfit business decisions because of your need to preserve capital (like offer deep discounts on product so you can afford the next grain order, for example). My advice is to total up a number for your property, FF&E (furniture, fixtures, and equipment), and the renovation/build-out. Then add 30 percent to that. That's a safe start.

2. **How much cash do I need to close a loan (if needed) and for working capital?**
3. **Do I qualify for an SBA 504 Loan? Reach out to your local Certified Development Company (CDC) that typically administers SBA loans to see if you qualify.**
4. **Where will my funding come from, and what will be the valuation of the company?**

Chapter 11
Sizing up the Brewery

Reed Odeneal[1]

DON'T FALL INTO the trap of undersizing your success.

We've all heard the stories about the enthusiastic startups who begin their journey on a nanosystem and struggled to keep their heads above water, or the halfhearted businesses who piece together laborious frankenbrew setups in order to save on startup capital just to get things off the ground. While some have found success, nearly all of them will be unanimous in their regret for not planning their systems to be larger and designed to grow with their business.

It's happened to some of the best, too.

"People always ask me (about sizing) because I was a nano brewery," said Burial Beer Co. Co-Founder Doug Reiser. "I always say that it was a terrible decision. I don't think it's smart business for anybody. I'm not saying you need to start at 10,000 barrels, but you need to start with a plan to get the 10,000 barrels in your first two years if that's your number. Whatever your number is. If your number's 50,000, you should start at 5,000, and scale up pretty quick, building your marketplace. I don't think you should be there, day one. I think it's kind of a two-step process."

Annual Production Forecasting

Having an understanding of your estimated annual production is one of the principal questions you should be able to answer to help ensure long-term success for your business. This should have already happened from a financial standpoint as you do your budget and projections for lenders

---

[1] Reed Odeneal is the Director of Brewing Operations at Perfect Plain Brewing Co.

and investors, but on the equipment side it will enable you to better estimate how large of a brewhouse you will need, how many fermenters and brite tanks you will need, and which size glycol system will be required.

Selecting a System Size

Calculating an estimated system size based on this will put you in a comfortable position to easily reach your target production forecast starting out. You should plan for 50 brewing weeks per year.

Example: 1,000 BBL/Year

System Size (BBL)	Production Estimate	Brew Days Per Week
5	1000 bbls per year / 5 bbl system / 50 brewing weeks per year	4
7	1000 bbls per year / 7 bbl system / 50 brewing weeks per year	3.8
10	1000 bbls per year / 7 bbl system / 50 brewing weeks per year	2

Is the juice worth the squeeze? When it comes to labor, probably not: You must look at the labor component when selecting a brewhouse size. Properly sized startups brew two to three times per week during the first several years in operation. If you start out brewing on undersized equipment, trading a higher frequency of brew days for expensive labor hours, your labor costs will rise significantly, stifling the opportunity to grow.

Calculating Cellar Capacity

Aside from selecting a proper brewhouse size, cellar space – your capacity for fermentation and maturation in fermentation tanks and brite beer vessels – can become a bottleneck in your production pipeline or a critical part of your overall success. This will greatly depend on the mix styles and maturation processes you plan to employ on an annual basis. While it's common to start out with equal-sized fermentation vessels, many taproom-focused breweries can easily double- or even triple-batch into larger vessels as demand and business growth increases. Floorspace and labor costs will play a major role in your cellar capacity, but understanding your cellar capacity needs is another principal question you should be able to answer in your overall brewery plan.

Here are some basics:

- Turnaround for most ales: 14 days
- Turnaround for most lagers: 28 days
- Cycles per year per fermenter for most ales: 25 (50 brewing weeks/14-day fermentation)
- Cycles per year per fermenter for most lagers: 12.5 (50 brewing weeks/28-day fermentation)

With your annual production forecast and system size, you should be able to easily establish a ballpark estimate for your cellar capacity.

Example: 1,000 BBL/Year, 10 BBL Brewhouse (70% Ales, 30% Lagers)

Production	Estimate	Capacity Requirement (Barrels)
Ales: 700 BBL	700 bbls per year / 25 cycles per year per fermenter	28
Lagers: 300 BBL	300 bbls per year / 12.5 cycles per year per fermenter	24

This means the total capacity requirement is 52 barrels. Based on this example and with a 10 bbl brewhouse, you would need to acquire 6x10bbl fermentation vessels to comfortably achieve your target annual production forecast.

Planning for Growth Proper sizing for a microbrewery should always allow for future expansion. Limiting your growth by undersizing and underoptimizing your brewhouse and tank space can be a costly mistake, and planning for expansion is critical if the budget can accommodate it.

Infrastructure Growth   Building for a larger infrastructure from the beginning can save you thousands of dollars down the road when you need to expand. You'll thank yourself later if you identify areas where you can extend critical infrastructure to utilize in the future. Consider the following:

- Extend floor drains when you first cut your concrete in areas where you want to add future fermentation and brite vessels.
- Don't forget about the electrical requirements. Install additional outlets (properly gauged wiring) where any future infrastructure will need to expand.
- Extend your glycol header loop and install additional valves that you can leave shut for future fermentation vessels and brite tanks.
- Plan your glycol chiller capacity for at least three years down the road.

Be Smart about Space   Space requirements will vary greatly from brewery to brewery and in a taproom brewery model, there is even more variability to consider. A common theme for brewery business owners when heading into years two and three is figuring out how to handle production growth with a limited building footprint. Undersize and you'll quickly become crowded for floorspace; oversize and you'll do more than bleed capital – you'll waste valuable square footage that can be used for the rest of your business.

Things to Consider for Space Utilization
- You probably need more storage than you think. Things like kegs, packaging, raw materials, freezers, refrigerators, replacement parts, tools, forklifts, pallet jacks, and spent grain can take up shocking amounts of space.
- You probably can't have enough cold storage.
- Brite tanks take up less square footage than kegs stacked two high.

Planning and administratively managing the back-of-house at a taproom-focused brewery model can look different than your traditional large production, distribution-heavy breweries. You still have to manage the major, important pieces like forecasting, batch scheduling, safety training, equipment maintenance schedules, and inventory, but in a business model where you live by your taproom, there are even more things you should consider. Here, we'll take a look at some of the things you should do from day one to set yourself up for success in the back of house.

Keeping It All Together: Brewery Management Software   Breweries, like all businesses, need systems in place to help them make informed decisions. Batch forecasting, state and federal excise taxes, batch tracking, raw materials inventory, personnel scheduling, product sales data . . . the list goes on and on. Brewery Management Software (BMS) acts as a source of truth for your brewery, consolidating information from an array of inputs, documents, clipboards, napkins, and much more. The opportunity to be "eyes on glass" and make real-time and calculated decisions about your business just isn't possible without a management system designed for breweries.

Tying into Your Taproom: Brewing for Programming   In a taproom-focused brewery model, driving revenue through programming, events, and festivals is a key component to early success. Integrate your brewing schedule and batch planning with your programming calendar from the get-go to give your patrons an immersive experience. A shared calendar with reminders set three months in advance can give you enough time to plan a special beer release, prepare a one-off pilot batch, or order seasonal ingredients for use in a beer for an approaching holiday. At Perfect Plain, we've found success with this simple reminder system that we check when we sit down to do our batch planning and raw material orders. There will be more on programming your taproom later in the book.

Hot Tip: We've had a lot of success utilizing Sabco's brite vessels for preparing one-off kegs for special events like birthdays, private parties, fundraisers, and so on.

Chapter 12

The Wonderful World of Permitting and Zoning

BEFORE YOU SKIP this chapter because it sounds un-fun, beware.

Many people opening breweries have figuratively done what you're about to do. And it has cost them a lot of money. And stress. And time. We have friends in this business who know this all too well.

I'm just glad I paid attention to a few of these things as we opened Perfect Plain.

Shopping for equipment was more fun. Finding a location was more fun. Closing the loan was more fun. But we saved a ton of money by understanding the circumstances, and the path to victory to getting our place opened ahead of time was just as rewarding.

Circumstances are wildly different based on your situation, but one thing you can count on is that you'll be required to deal with permitting, city planning, review boards, licenses, permissions, and polices.

When I speak at college or entrepreneurial courses, one of the most common questions I get is, "What was the biggest mistake you made getting your place open?" It was the keg washer. The *damn* keg washer.

But I'm proud to say that we were never tripped up in permitting, in planning, and only *slightly* by the fire marshal. Our secret was being proactive in understanding what was in front of us. We didn't want for someone to stop us; we asked questions. We had meetings with officials.

Here's the key not to miss: First-time business owners get lulled into this false sense that the government should be telling them things they should know in advance. Don't fall into that trap. That would be nice, but the reality is that if you didn't get confirmation of planning, or fire code, or how much parking you are supposed to have for your type of zoning, that's on your inability both to know and to ask the right questions *proactively*.

Instead of being reactionary, meeting with the right people and asking the right questions was more than worth our time. Even better, when city/county/state officials see you care enough to do your homework, they're suddenly a little more understanding when something goes wrong or gets missed.

Here's a sampling of the list of permissions we needed to open Perfect Plain:

- Federal TTB approval
- Florida Department of Business and Professional Regulation and Florida Division of Alcoholic Beverages and Tobacco, approval for two permits: brewing and a beer/wine license (and again six months later for our liquor license)
- County business license
- City business license, required by the city (To get that, we needed permission to sell beer within 500 feet of a church and a letter in writing from First Presbyterian Church.)
- Bathroom counts approved by city permitting (Because we were altering the building from a print shop to a brewery, all electrical, plumbing, bathrooms, etc., had to be brought up to code since the use was changing.)
- As renovated, appraisal had to come back at a certain dollar amount to execute the loan with our bank
- State licensing approval of all owners, which included full profiles and fingerprints
- City of Pensacola Architectural Review Board approval on our signage out front (We are located in a "review district" in the heart of downtown, so all exterior improvements – paint color, signage, lighting – must be approved. We had to go there three times.)
- Clearance on parking requirements since we were downtown and licensing as a bar (Pensacola is rather behind the times on parking requirements in urban areas. Most populated areas already have or are starting to get rid of parking requirements in entertainment areas, but definitely ask about this.)
- Mechanical, electrical, and plumbing approval to get building permits; turbulent but relatively unscathed
- Lease with the Florida Department of Transportation in order to use outdoor seating on the sidewalk (We needed to execute this

lease because we are located on a state road. We had to hire a surveyor to get exact coordinates of the space and it took about 100 e-mails to complete. We are charged $1,000 annually for the lease.)

- Fire marshal sign-off (The day before we opened, despite the fact that we sprinklered the building, and despite no previous mention of this, they required us to put in a $4,000 fire call box that automatically calls the fire department when smoke is detected. We paid extra and it was installed four hours before we opened.)

I share this list with you, first, selfishly, because it's cathartic to look at all the shit Reed and I had to do to get this place open. Less selfishly, I share this list to get your brain working about questions you need to ask. I'm not going to spend a lot of time going through too many specifics on issues we ran into, because policies, rules, and procedures vary so widely from one city or municipality to another that our individual stories and fixes may be completely inapplicable for you. But hopefully this list gets your brain moving on topics you should be asking about.

Here are some steps that helped us.

In the city of Pensacola, each Wednesday at 9 a.m. at City Hall, all the important parties for small business gather in the same room to allow citizens to ask questions and discuss a property they plan on buying/leasing, finding out what's required from zoning to building permits to fire code. There's even an economic development person with the city in the meeting in case there are any incentives or grants available based on your industry or other consideration.

I went to this meeting no fewer than four times before we purchased our building. It took me, on average, 30 minutes each time. But I saved countless dollars and hours knowing ahead of time that we needed fire sprinklers for the building, rather than learning after the fact. I knew I would have to get permission from our nearby church. Imagine if we bought our building and were ready to open and then the church refused to grant permission?

Ask your local governing body if they do something like this in your town for small businesses. Obviously, the more details you have about architectural plans, the more impactful these meetings will be. At a minimum, have the details about a building you plan to put in an offer on so the specifics of that location can be analyzed.

If your government doesn't do a streamlined approach, it's something you can arrange yourself. Call the relevant people, and heck, if there's a conference room at city hall, get them all in the same room yourself.

The three most important:

- Planning and zoning
- Fire marshal/fire chief
- City permitting (mechanical/electrical/plumbing)
- Health department (if you plan on serving food)

In addition, the best thing you can do to ensure you don't miss a step is to ask someone else who has recently gone through this process in your community. It doesn't have to be a brewery – a bar whose food offering, or lack thereof, matches yours would be the most similar.

All of this information also saves you money with your build-out. It leads to fewer change orders when you and/or your general contractor understand what is expected in order to adhere to all rules and regulations.

Bring this list of key questions to ask before you reach a point of no return:

- What are our bathroom requirements based on our building occupancy?
- What will our zoning be? Is there a specific brewery zoning or a bar zoning we fall under? What are the differences?
- What requirements do we have under that zoning? Do we need permission from a school or a church?
- We plan on our taproom being (enter square footage here). How many bathrooms will it require us to build?
- What are our handicap accessibility requirements?
- What are our fire requirements for the brewery in particular? How do our requirements change if we invest in a fire suppression/sprinkler system? (For example, we were able to have an open-air brewery with no walls separating the taproom because we sprinklered the building.)
- Do we need a lease from a government body to use a sidewalk as outdoor seating? What are the other requirements?
- Is our location in a review or approval district for anything outside of standard city permitting and zoning?

CHAPTER 13

What to Ask Your Architect and Contractors

WHEN YOU ARE borrowing money, paying a mortgage, or paying a lease, time becomes a significant amount of money. It's important to know what's going on at your property and it's important to prevent as many delays as possible.

I'm going to clue you in on the world's worst secret. You are going to get delayed on something. Probably multiple things. If you never got delayed and your construction or renovation finished on time and under budget, please allow me to congratulate you for being the first brewery ever to accomplish this feat.

This is me smiling before I knew how much work I had in front of us to turn this old print shop into a craft brewery.

A in progress.

Again, while it's easy to point fingers during these delays, doing your homework and understanding your property, your project, and your relationships with your contractor (if needed) and vendors will inevitably save you time and money. Here are my nine keys to maximizing your time and effort to save you a ton in the long run.

1. **Set deadlines up front.** Anyone who has been through a construction or renovation project knows the old saying "twice as expensive, twice as long." While there can be unforeseen delays out of their control (e.g. permitting, inspections), if you don't agree to completion deadlines with architects, contractors, and engineers in advance, rest assured you won't be saying, "Wow, they got that done a lot faster than I thought!"

2. **What's important in a contractor:** 1) You can get them on the phone. 2) They are flexible with change. 3) They are a steward of your money. They treat it like it's their own. Make sure you discuss these with the contractors bidding on your project. Perhaps you don't think you can afford a contractor? Before you assume

not hiring one is the way to go, factor in the additional time (and lost revenue opportunity, additional interest paid on loans, etc.) to complete your project.

3. **Know your building.** If you are renovating a building you bought or leased, how many gallons per minute are coming in for your current water service? How many BTUs does your current gas line have? Those can be adjusted, but likely they come with significant fees. What kind of shape are the big-ticket items in? Most common would be HVAC, bathrooms that comply with the Americans with Disabilities Act (ADA), and any city/local code.

4. **Photos, photos, photos.** While we all like to believe we're great with words, when working with architects and contractors, nothing compares to photos of concepts, looks, and designs you like. I stored up a library of photos. Some had just one little thing I liked, maybe the way they designed the bar top. It may just be a piece of signage or gooseneck lighting you think looks cool. (I remember Oxbow's back bar was one we referenced a lot.) Nab photos of all of those things, even if you like one facet of a photo and don't like anything else. If you don't have visuals, you'll be left scrambling to explain your vision to your architect and contractor.

5. **Do they have brewery experience?** By now, thanks to this national boom in craft, most cities of a decent size have seen new breweries built. Finding architects, engineers, and contractors who have done a brewery before is an obvious advantage. Don't need to tell you that, right? But let me explain a subtler reason it's important. When a plumber has little or no experience cutting a long trench drain, for example, because of their own lack of experience, they will charge you more money to build it. Why? When a subcontractor is unsure how long something will take to do, they're going to overestimate the time needed to make sure they are covered and won't lose money. Having experience with all facets of your project that are uncommon in most businesses – think trench drains, sloped floors, glycol loops – will not only give you piece of mind but will save you dollars. If there is no one in your immediate area with brewery experience, don't hesitate to call someone from a neighboring area who does. That extra drive time may be worth it. Don't wait for a contractor – start looking into vendors who have specific experience in what you are seeking to do.

6. **Make reference checks on your contractors and key subcontractors – and not just with their previous customers.** The general contractor, plumber, and electrician will have to deal with your local municipality for inspections and approvals. How familiar are your subcontractors with your city inspection officials? What kind of reputation do they have for quality work from the city/municipality point of view? A phone call to city hall or your county office is worthwhile.

7. **Open book?** Always ask if a general contractor will do a deal "open book." That means that you and the general contractor agree to a percentage fee of the entire project (10% is standard in our area), but the contractor will share all invoices of the subcontractors with you. That's a much more transparent way to work than for the GC to project a cost for the project, then become subconsciously motivated to spend less money with subcontractors only to keep more for his or her own company.

8. **Be present during the construction.** Again, this seems obvious, but it's important. Make sure you are around as the project gets executed. I can't count how many times a subcontractor moved an outlet, changed out a light fixture location, made an adjustment to a drain, or the like, all on the fly, even when we had agreed on something different during the design phase. Why? Sometimes you need to see it in person to really know what it looks like and you may not like it as planned. Don't just assume that if it's on the plan, you'll like it. Thanks to a great contractor – Kevin Hagen of H&H Building Group, who was flexible and easy to get ahold of – we made plenty of little changes that would have been much more punitive had we not been in touch and on site on a regular basis. Plus (and this is just my theory), I think your subcontractors are likely to work a little faster when they know the person paying them is around every so often.

9. **Check into sustainable design.** Could you power your building partly or completely with solar? Sounds daunting, but costs and local incentive programs are making that more and more achievable. We didn't open that way, but Perfect Plain is currently looking into going solar. It's not only good for the environment, but in some cases you can get your money back in a matter of 5–10 years as well as go on the grid with your power company with the capability to sell back to them any excess energy created. It may be too expensive for a startup to handle, but the phone call and site visit from a professional costs nothing.

The fruits of our labor.

Chapter 14

Best Practices Q&A: Jester King Founder Jeffrey Stuffings

ALMOST A DECADE ago, Jeffrey Stuffings left his law degree behind and found his calling on a four-acre plot in Texas Hill Country, west of Austin. That's where he began creating what would become one of the nation's most celebrated farmhouse breweries. I think it's one of the biggest compliments in our industry to be considered what I call a *Pilgrimage Brewery*, where you don't have to rely on a prime location. Instead, no matter how remote your location, people come seek you out.

I did the same thing. I took a trip to Jester King in 2018 and was – like so many others – blown away with the brewery, the delicious spontaneous ferm beers, and just the feel and experience. But, as a fledgling brewery owner, I was just as impressed with all of Jester King's back office. Thinking a place this laid-back and beautiful wouldn't be anywhere near the level of data nerd I am, I saw whiteboards showing sales numbers, bonuses and bonus goals for employees, so many things being tracked and measured – the kind of business creativity, transparency, and leadership that can keep a brewery business strong.

And it's been strong. Now up to 60 acres of land, Jester King also has an operational farm – goats, grapes, and all – a restaurant, a brewery, a taproom, and a private event space.

I talked with him about finding that balance of creativity and business – how to manage it, how to cascade it to staff, what he's still trying to improve at Jester King, and what he looks for in a strong taproom experience.

D.C. Reeves: Do you remember the moment at Jester King when you departed from the "hobby" mentality and moved into the "how to sustain a successful craft beer business" mentality? And

what was that process like, dealing with that mental shift that so many breweries are going through, or will go through soon?

Jeffrey Stuffings: Yes. I think at first, certainly during the startup days, and then really into, I'd say, practically the first five or six years in the business, our focus was almost completely on making beer, making quality beer, interesting beer that has an interesting story behind it and telling that story. From a retail perspective, it was fairly easy at the time. From 2013 to 2016 or early '17, it was pretty much just open the door, whatever we have available would sell out. Then we're closed for the afternoon, and then see you next weekend! And there wasn't a whole lot of thought behind the retail side of it.

And then things started to grow. We expanded to include a restaurant, an event center, a small farm, and all of a sudden we have twice as many employees, and more moving parts, and it dawned on me: Your job is no longer to be the best brewer or production manager; it's to be the best business person you can be. I've got to pivot to learn how to manage an organization. I guess if I really was dead set, "I'm going to stick to brewing beer, I'm not going to worry about this," then I would have had to hire someone to do it, because it became very apparent that it needed to be done.

I would say it was kind of that realization around 2016, 2017 for me that I've got to start learning how to operate a small business, and then it was kind of a re-education where I'm trying to read all the books I can. Finding other successful business people to pick their brain, and then trying to mimic other successful organizations. I like to joke that Jolly Pumpkin in Michigan gave us inspiration to start making beer. And then we started drawing inspiration from another Ann Arbor business called Zingerman's, which is just now this community of business that touches on all things, food, drinks, fermentation, and arts and goods.

It just became apparent to me that we were becoming this little community of businesses out here at Jester King and, for it to run right, someone needed to figure out how to manage people, how to manage our organization, creating priorities, manage finance. I felt like we have good quality. But we don't have great finance, and we don't have great . . . well, I don't want to knock the customer service side of it; we weren't great and we're still not. But at least you could say we're focused a lot more on those other pillars now than we were for the first five or six years of our business.

DC: How important is the data piece to you? Are there certain metrics that are more important to you? Which numbers speak to you the most?

JS: Sure. It's huge. Going back to Zingerman's, you know, we moved to adopt their system of management, which I think has had a number of benefits for us over the last, roughly, two years. We've started paying attention to leading indicators we can focus on and not just the trailing ones. And being able to actually do things proactively to move those bottom-line numbers, finding the levers that can have the biggest impact.

One of the ones we've really started to focus on is ways that we can drive on-site draught sales, as we've experienced a changing market, where bottle releases aren't as impactful as they were a couple of years ago. Meanwhile, our area is growing tremendously around us, the southwest Austin area, so finding ways to essentially increase on-site draught is one of our critical numbers.

Going back to open book management, we're still two years into running it. We're still tweaking it constantly and getting better at it. But I'd say we have, like, our all-company numbers and we go over all the managers. We have this meeting on Fridays to go over all the numbers and see how we did for the previous week, how we're doing for the quarter, how we're doing for the year.

We set up goals around the numbers and then a reward system, a financial bonus reward or revenue sharing around hitting our numbers. It's based on the philosophy that you take care of covering your operating expenses first and then benefits, improvements, shareholder equity, taxes. And then, if anything is left, then that money is shared between our employees and the company in form of a revenue-sharing bonus.

And then we have all our department numbers as well. We try to avoid the notion that if everything's important then nothing's important. So, we just pick out two or three things per department that we're going to focus on. For instance, for production, one of the things we've noticed is that we can label by hand. We have very small production volume. But if we can get our stuff together across all the other departments, where the labels are in, the beer's ready, and we can actually label in-line, as opposed to packaging beer and then putting into case cartons, taking it out, labeling it and putting it back in – then yeah, we see a direct benefit to our bottom line. So, every department has its numbers and we set up miniature goals around them. We have our main company bonus, and then we set up miniature goals around – or rewards, I should say – around the department-critical numbers.

And then all that data is published. You'll have your simplified versions of it on the boards that you saw. And we've tried to make it more digestible. This is a scenario where we haven't done a tremendous job yet, teaching people in the organization how to read a balance sheet, read a profit and loss statement, all that info. We have other information published electronically, on a weekly basis, and then we have two meetings a year, which everyone is required to attend, where we just go over all the finances for the previous two quarters.

But everyone, from our managers to our dishwashers, all that information passed to them and reviewed with them at least twice per year. We can see so many little examples through that transparency, that people just react so much better when things change. For instance, with our production team, you know, they've been able to feed me data on, "This beer's great. We should still make it more popular. But given how much it takes to make, and given how much demand that there is, we should do 20 barrel (batches) instead of 60."

This is stuff we never would have been able to uncover without opening up the books and showing everyone how this is run financially.

DC: With the growth in our industry, has the sharpening of the business mind of your typical brewery owner increased? Or perhaps the "taboo" effect of talking about business and finances and such has decreased in recent years as the craft beer market has saturated? I asked Doug Reiser from Burial Beer Co. – also a former attorney turned brewery owner – the same question.

JS: Yes, from my personal experience on that, getting out of a white-collar law firm environment, where I did not find the work and the culture appealing, and with Jester we're going to create this pirate ship or never-neverland environment where we're going to engage in creative beer making and not have anything smack of corporate life. And, when you have five or six people working together, that's very easy to maintain. But as we've grown and now have approximately 65 employees, this is not realistic. You're just going to piss off a bunch of people because they don't know what's expected of them; they don't know what they're doing and there's mass confusion with their jobs.

We felt it has been absolutely a necessity to implement more structure to what we do and have clear guideline expectations for everyone in the organization. I think we still have fun. I think we still keep that spirit. But it's different.

Maybe it's just because this is what I'm interested in these days, so it maybe manifests itself in the conversations that I have, but yeah, I think there's definitely more interest in talking about the business of beer. I mean, a lot of people will come up to me, like, "Hey, I see you've been talking about open-book management. I mean, what is that? How can I do that for my brewery?"

I definitely do feel it's less of a taboo subject. When we started doing stuff like this, I personally felt, like, oh man, maybe I'm kind of selling out here. Maybe I'm starting to be the man, whatever. And now, I just don't feel that. I think it's responsible to be doing these things and having these conversations.

DC: Yeah, from my personal experience going to Jester King, what you guys do better than almost anybody is to create that organic experience for your customers while still having a strong focus on the health of the company. You guys balance that probably better than anyone. Have there been challenges to that? To be data driven and to be business driven, and I think sometimes people feel you have to choose one or the other. Like you said, "Am I becoming 'the man?'"

How do you balance that awesome, organic passion and experience with still doing those important business things that make you sustainable?

JS: So, I think we have our core values. And that's just another example of something we didn't even bother putting on paper or trying to articulate. So, really within the last two years we've grown up tremendously. We still have a way to go. But we outlined our first value, and I guess they're all co-equals, but the first was engage creativity. Walking in the door, you're presented with our core values and you're told part of your job is to be creative.

And that can manifest itself, obviously, in different ways, and different positions or different responsibilities. But this is going to be a creative process for you, and we want it to be fun and interesting and alive.

And I think continually we're still making the same beer, in the same way and with the same philosophy. So, with our kitchen, we can do all kinds of these interesting dishes, work with cool ingredients, try different types of fermentations in the kitchen. Granted, we have a fairly large kitchen and customer base for our restaurant, but it's small enough where we can be creative.

Brewing is the same thing. We're just doing about 2,000 barrels a year. A lot of one-off projects, with fun ingredients or techniques or barrels. And, in a way, none of that has really changed. Everything is still stirred by hand. It's just that there's a lot of stuff now. Instead of just making beer, now there's all these other things.

And, so, for us to be effective and to sustain this creativity, there has to be more structure, especially across departments where we've been able to promote it to our staff.

So, I think that more and more people here are realizing that we need to pay attention to what's most important now; what's most important for the year; what's required of everyone to get there; how are we doing based on these numbers? Then it's just going to be a cluster, and it's not going to work. And it's all just going to crumble inward.

So, I think that's been the pitch. For us to sustain, we want to engage creativity. How do we sustain it? We have to be mindful of financial sustainability, energy sustainability, and environmental sustainability, both for the broader environment but particularly our ranch. For instance, are we going to be able to have the resources we need to be a business that stands the test of time? And, so, I think people see that if we want A, we've got to have B. So that's what we're trying to preach.

DC: If you were starting Jester King in 2019, what would be the first two or three things you would do, or you think would be important to your success?

JS: Yes, I think I would try to just be very authentic and transparent in what you're seeking to do, whatever it is. And try to have at least enough unique character to where it doesn't feel like you're jumping on the bandwagon or coattails of whatever else is happening in the industry.

Occasionally, I'll see breweries come along that, if they aren't totally novel, at least they're an interesting twist on something, and you can tell there was some thought behind it.

For instance, our former head brewer is opening a new brewery in Texas and it's going to be a very authentic expression of what he's into. And, I think, doing that on a small-scale basis, where you're not trying to play the regional game, is the right way to go about it.

Brewers Association data essentially shows that at the regional level, there's no growth. And so, it's about finding a geographical area in which he can really just make honest, authentic beers that are not just following a trend.

Ultimately, I would just say start with the taproom experience. I mean, why do people go to breweries? What would you want to experience? Why would you go there? You know, is it going to be just a sterile environment, with white walls and bright lights?

So, I would try to be thoughtful in terms of having a unique character that reflects who you are and what you value. So, I think it's kind of an interesting blend between reflecting your own character and personality and also being in a controlled environment where people would actually want to spend their free time.

Beer wise, I would probably focus on very simple, drinkable beers. Simple, honest beers that can be enjoyed over the course of a session with friends. And then, of course, experimentation as a secondary component of that. And then, I guess, identifying a place that could use something that, if not brand new or novel, is at least relatively unique for the environment. And then, just having enough character and soul and not being just another cardboard cutout of something that's already there.

DC: What dictates a great taproom experience for you?

JS: I would say a comfortable environment that has some unique character to it. It doesn't have to have an outright theme. But something that denotes what you're about, what you believe in, like, what it says to you. Was it fun? I mean, the reason people are going to breweries is, presumably, to have fun with friends.

Sam Calagione's book *Brewing up a Business* is one of the first ones I read and thought it was really good. He said, "Let your freak flag fly." And I think that's true.

Also, the quality's got to be there. If I walk in and the beer is all diacetyl and out of balance and the food sucks, then that's almost, like, you're done. You don't even get past go.

So, quality has got to be there, first and foremost. And I think empathetic warmth from the staff and communicating to your guests that you're on their side. You get it, you have empathy for this person. They probably had a long work week, and they probably don't have a lot of free time. And being actually grateful that they chose to spend it with you, approaching it from that mentality. Quality, staff, and character.

DC: Most people just starting a craft brewery, or those who have one in its infancy, probably think that nationally renowned breweries like yours don't have issues or concerns. I'm sure you have some. What are you seeking to improve right now?

JS: I would say a couple of items are big priorities right now.

We expanded in 2018 from brewery and fledgling farm to brewery, slightly more robust farm, events center, and a restaurant. And we've made good strides with the restaurant; we still have work to do but made good strides. We're giving kind of a long runway to the event business and we have not really seen the returns from that portion off of what we acquired. So, I would say an event business that's booked out and is making really good margins off of catering and beer sales to people having on-site events.

The other focus would be really tightening up front-of-house roles and responsibilities. We've got a good legacy staff, but the ask of them, for years, was just to essentially roll up the door and ring in sales. And that was it – the release would sell out by Saturday afternoon or Sunday afternoon. And then some customers would stick around and hang out. But now, going back to what I was saying before about empathetic warmth and hospitality, actually providing experiences, anticipating customers' needs, that's where we have to go next.

So, we're not there yet, but we're in the process of redefining all of our front-of-house roles and what they mean, and what their responsibilities are. We started a couple of months ago as if we're just starting from scratch and kind of redefined everything and haven't even formally communicated that to our staff. But we're really engaged in the training that's going to make it work. So, front-of-house expectations and training is a big focus of ours.

And then the third one, I would say, would be line management and efficiency for our back-of-house. You know, we took over a kitchen that – no fault to the previous owners – but it just didn't aspire to be anything more than very simple, here are four different kinds of pizzas and salads and garlic knots and that was it. I don't know if they were comfortable or not, but the reality is that they would get extremely bogged down and backed up with their order-taking time, their preparation times. They had no mechanism of food delivery, other than somebody with a broken cell phone just texting people.

So, we're in the process of reconfiguring our kitchen, maximizing the functionality of a new POS system and making it so that, instead of waiting 90 minutes to get your food at our peak times, maybe it's now 45 minutes instead. I remember one of the business books saying something like, "Don't even think about growing until you are actually optimizing your existing business." And we're still, I would say, one or two years away till I think we're at that point.

So, yeah. Major front-of-house and back-of-house priorities. If it sounds like I'm talking like a restaurateur, yeah, that's where we find ourselves.

I'll throw in one more that actually is more beer focused. I already alluded to this – we would just brew whatever we wanted; if it sounded cool, we'd do it; pay no attention, really, to what it cost, how much we think we'd sell, how much we could make, what the margins are. And so, we've gotten various software now, and we are actually tracking the margins on all these beers, factoring labor costs, assigning a value – time value of money for aging these beers. And we're discovering that it doesn't necessarily make sense to tie up a 60-barrel tank with a fruit refermentation when you can actually put a simple, hoppy, bitter farmhouse ale in there and keg it out and serve it at our bar.

We're still making some of these beers that are our most popular ones, but we're putting them in a foeder, or we're putting them in a tank and making 10, 20 barrels instead of 60, which has been weird to us, that making less of our most popular beers is actually more profitable.

Stuff I'm telling you right now we just uncovered at the end of last quarter (early 2019). So, actually, putting analysis, thought process, and financial analysis into our production schedule is something we're just now doing for the first time ever.

I guess that'd be my list of three or four things that I will hope to have gone well as we get into the next two years.

DC: Prediction time: Where do you think the industry will be in five years? What will we be talking about in 2024?

JS: In terms of macro trends I think we'll be talking about how we are kind of stabilizing out. I think it's going to get kind of rough out there. I really do.

I think we already are starting to look back on – to steal a phrase from (Stone Brewing CEO) Greg Koch – the kind of irrational exuberance of growth expansion by volume. And I think we'll be talking about how there was a bubble that developed that, if not popped, at least started to deflate a little bit.

I personally feel like consumer interests have, understandably, come to also include other types of artisan alcoholic beverages, as well as other recreational drugs or intoxicants, like cannabis or whatever, and that we jumped the gun on the craft boom as an industry. And I think we're kind of coming back to earth.

But, with that said, I think more positively we'll be speaking about how we've returned to 1845 [pre-Prohibition], when there were still a ton of breweries and they were serving fresh beer to their neighborhood. So, I think we will still see a lot of openings. I think we'll see that gap between openings and closures start to narrow some.

And I think the biggest trend – no surprise – everyone's going to be focusing on it . . . I look at the openings happening right now in Austin, and for instance, an awesome restaurant is putting in a 3-barrel system to make some beer at their little bakery.

And, so, I think we'll be talking about how we jumped the gun in the industry but ultimately found ourselves in a good place.

DC: Perhaps it becomes a bit of ironic self-selection and we don't have to worry so much about brewers or breweries misrepresenting the craft beer name by creating something of poor quality. Maybe they filter out because of all the options?

JS: Yeah. On a positive note, though, I remember people like Sam Calagione talking about how we want to create a landscape where we'll go from a country that, instead of being dominated by a couple of giant breweries, is full of life and color, figuratively speaking, when it comes to beer. And I think that we're seeing that now. I go and visit my side of the family in rural Iowa, and you're actually seeing some really great breweries in little pockets of towns that most people have never even heard of. So, from that standpoint, I think we've done an amazing job as an industry, and we'll be celebrating that.

Part III

The Keys to Success: Leadership and Company Culture

THIS SECTION IS the secret sauce of microbreweries.

When I travel the country, I rarely find breweries that invest financially and time-wise in their company culture, employee engagement, and creating a great place to work. There are so many valuable reverberating effects of this investment: better service, less turnover, less spillage, fewer mistakes, no lawsuits, and seeing great attitudes in your establishment.

Read that list, then ask yourself: How much more time do you spend on recipe generation? Distribution logistics? Those are valuable, and it's human nature to shy away from those "softer" investments. Why? It makes us look in the mirror as owners and managers, change our behavior, and be accountable for keeping up with something we're not as comfortable with.

Let's get comfortable.

I believe that this section of the book, more than any other, can set your brewery apart in your community. You'll be doing what few have learned to do. A great company culture will change every part of your life for the better.

Chapter 15

The Start to a Successful Brewery: Keys to Strong Leadership

I'M A BREWERY owner, but one thing that has been vital in our success is having an understanding boss. This brewery wouldn't exist without Quint Studer, who not only was willing to be flexible with my hours as his chief of staff to allow me to invest time in the brewery, but also taught me so much about employee culture and opening a business.

Quint is a household name in healthcare. After a successful career turning around the customer satisfaction at two large hospitals – Holy Cross Hospital in Chicago and Baptist Hospital in Pensacola – Quint began Studer Group, a national healthcare consulting firm, in 2000. He owned and operated the company for 16 years, becoming the gold standard in the industry. His company worked with every health system you've heard of, and if you know someone in healthcare, they probably know him or Studer Group, implement some of their teachings (AIDET is a popular one), or have read one of his many books on healthcare or leadership.

One of the biggest influences Quint has had on me, both philosophically and tactically, is striving for strong employee engagement. When Quint was brought into Holy Cross and Baptist, he was handed the same problem: terrible customer satisfaction. Healthcare at the time invested little into the customer experience. You needed a doctor, they had one. That was it.

Many hospitals – and breweries are no different – attempted to improve customer satisfaction by treating symptoms. Yelp reviews no good? We'll offer more specials! We'll do more events! We'll respond to reviews! We'll offer more things!

Problem was, that never solved it. The secret sauce is that strong customer satisfaction is completely, and directly, tied to strong employee engagement. If your employees love to work for you and your company, you will have happy customers. Period.

The next several chapters will give tactics and tools to help achieve strong hiring processes, leadership, employee engagement, onboarding, and more.

Leadership is the top of the employee engagement pyramid, whether that's the owner, CEO, or general manager. There has to be complete cultural and ethical alignment at the top or the rest will be impossible.

The leadership of your organization will be the most important hires you make. It's worth investing time, energy, and sometimes extra dollars for a supremely strong candidate; just think about all the extra sleep you will get when you know how strong those folks minding the operation are.

Studer shared his keys to being a great leader in the *Pensacola News Journal* in 2018, discussing the 12 things that make people want to follow someone. Be sure to share this with other ownership and your current managers and employees.

1. **First and foremost: trustworthiness.** If followers can't trust you to do what you say you're going to do and to do right by them and the company, they will never really follow you. Part of them will always hold back, second guess, and seek to protect themselves.
2. **A clear and inspiring vision for the future.** If you don't know where you're going – and can't clearly articulate that vision – how can followers follow? They can't. By definition, followers are following you to some destination. The goals you set for them are simply mile markers on the journey.
3. **Courage and willingness to act.** It can be a scary world out there. People want to follow someone who is not afraid to make the tough decisions and take action. Of course, they know you can make mistakes. Anyone can. But most followers realize instinctively that life favors boldness and action, not hesitancy and waffling.
4. **An appreciation for the ideas and viewpoints of followers.** Great leaders really want the input of their team. They are fully aware that they don't and can't know everything. On the other hand, great

leaders generally seek consent, not consensus. Waiting for every-one to agree can paralyze you to the point that nothing gets done.

5. **Emphasis on the why.** The best leaders constantly tell employees not just what to do, but why they're being asked to do it. We all need to feel a sense of purpose and to believe our work is meaning-ful. When people get the why – the difference they're making in the customer's life – they're far more likely to buy into what you're asking them to do.

6. **Ability to give clear, simple, detailed instructions.** The why is only the beginning. Followers also need to know what, how, when, and where. No one likes uncertainty and vagueness. Nor do they like the feeling that they're being purposely left in the dark. This creates anxiety and sends people down the wrong path. Great leaders are always in touch, checking in, clarifying, and asking, "What are your questions?"

7. **Transparency with the truth (even when it's bad news).** When you aren't transparent, people assume the worst. Their imagina-tions run away with them. They stew in anxiety rather than devot-ing their full attention to work. Treat followers like the adults they are. They can handle the truth.

8. **Consistent behavior/treating everyone fairly.** Consistently make decisions and hold people accountable based on clear goals and objective metrics. (This connects to how you evaluate perfor-mance. Subjectivity is a toxic force.)

9. **Humility.** Leadership is not always about being "right." Great leaders are more than happy to leverage the smart ideas of others and let others have the credit. Also, they are willing to say, "I was wrong." Followers can relate to leaders who are human and willing to admit to flaws and mistakes.

10. **Openness to critical feedback.** The humility I just mentioned should be obvious enough that people feel comfortable telling you that you've gone "off the grid" if necessary. You might even consider purposely saying something that doesn't make sense to see if someone will speak up. This is a good way to gauge the kind of culture you're creating.

11. **Respectfulness.** If you are frequently disrespectful to employees – belittling, bullying, yelling at, or attempting to manipulate them – they won't follow you. They may resentfully comply, but you will never get the best ideas and the fullest measure of effort from them.

12. **Gratitude.** People gladly follow you when you acknowledge their contributions and say thank you from time to time. This is why reward and recognition are so important.

I'll be the first to say I don't live up to all 12 of these. But I do try and keep them in front of me at all times and strive to include many in my daily works.

Within this world, what speaks most to me is encapsulated in these topics:

1. **Creating a sense of ownership.** I want our employees to feel as if they're owners or are treated as owners, not as if there is a caste system in our company. Employees are smart and understand that there are meetings among leaders that not every single employee can be involved in. But when their opinion is heard and truly valued on a regular basis, it's a powerful thing.

2. **Be transparent, even with financials.** Short of specific employee salary information or confidential employee transactions like probation and/or health situations, our company is wide open. Any bartender can ask to see our financials at any time, and we remind them of that. Each night, when our nightly report is sent out listing total revenue sold for that day, it goes to all employees. I want them to feel as informed and included as I am. To achieve transparency, know that efficient communication and effective cascading of information to staff is paramount.

Everything that this company will do begins with its ownership: how they act, how they respond, how they install structure in the company, how they hire, how they take care of their employees, and how they set the tone.

How many times have we heard someone say, "Man, I just can't find good help around here!" Sure, the economy in 2019 is booming, and craft alcohol sectors have been on the same plane. Finding good talent isn't easy. But when I hear how a brewery can't keep employees, I find that it may not be the employees to blame. More often than not it comes down to leadership and it comes down to proper hiring.

We'll show you how our hiring process works for us.

Chapter 16

How to Hire Well and Eliminate Turnover in Three Steps

Photo Credits: Jeremy Cook

I'm going to share a hiring process with you that will cultivate many great things within your company. This hiring process, if done correctly, produces better candidates, saves you money by limiting turnover, improves employee engagement, fosters an ownership culture throughout your staff, and improves your chances of a strong onboarding for new hires.

And crazier still, this process can save you money.

Packs a punch, right?

I call it three-step interviewing. I've made a few tweaks from what I've learned about this process, which is often used to hire CEOs or high-level executives, to develop this process for our industry.

Hiring Key: The Job Description

In the hustle of everyday operations, it would be easy to cut and paste someone else's job description from another brewery, fill the role as quickly as possible, and hold your breath.

But don't overlook the value of a sound job description.

When asked what he looks for in strong leaders, Dogfish Head's Sam Calagione said it starts before they're even brought in for an interview.

"I'd say it starts with a really well-articulated and exhaustively detailed job description," Calagione said. "Then at the bottom it should always say something like 'and other responsibilities as they may come up.' For any leader at this company, we all pitch in when audibles [last-minute changes] have to be made, but really starting with codifying what the job is. Documenting, codifying it in the language of your brand. If you're super irreverent and casual that can be conveyed, but at least it's again something that's on paper that everyone can reference and there can be less chance for crossed wires of expectations."

Ask around at other like-sized breweries for an example of their latest job description, then work off that to ensure that the description speaks to your needs, your brand, and your focus.

And while we're talking about a miniscule sample size, our employee retention has lapped the industry average. Many factors play key roles in that – culture, engagement, and others we'll address later – but none have the singular impact as hiring well.

We're fortunate in the craft beer industry that our standard applicant base, on average, will have more passion for our product and process than a typical restaurant or bar does.

Turnover is a hidden cash pit. According to the Center for Hospitality Research at Cornell University, turnover costs hospitality companies an average of $5,864 per employee. Most owners, busy with day-to-day-operations, don't think about those costs. But stop and think about the expense of new hires:

- All of the overtime hours or sacrifices made in production because of the missing staff member

- Hours it takes you and your leadership to sift through resumes, interview candidates, make hires
- Training time to onboard into your organization correctly, regardless of their skill level
- Mental strain and lowered morale of an overworked staff covering shifts (not financial, but a cost nonetheless)

Some of those have clear dollar figures attached, and some don't. Nonetheless, turnover is expensive, so when you think you're saving money by expediting your hiring process, or you refuse to buy a plane ticket for a potential hire because "it's too expensive," know that there is nothing regarding your staff that is more expensive than making a wrong hire. I guarantee that this process will save you thousands of dollars in the long run.

One warning before we begin. If you are going to adopt this process, it has to be followed religiously. And that means sacrifices. It means if you are an owner or leader in the organization, you're giving up the freedom to just hire whoever you want. If you undercut the process, you undercut the integrity of your hires, create double standards, and negatively impact company culture and morale. You'll understand why soon.

The three steps of this process are:

- The HR interview
- The technical interview
- The peer interview

Before Step 1: Vetting

At this point, leaders have an applicant pool and have sifted through to pick some clear frontrunners. Maybe there are five or six, maybe there is one clear-cut leader who stands out to you all.

Aside from the obvious like experience, skill set, and technical expertise, let me give you a few of my personal preferences of what I hope to see in job applications.

1. **No typos or blatant grammatical errors.** Yes, this is a pet peeve carryover from my journalism days. But follow me here. I believe that anyone who is being considered as a finalist for a job at our company should want it bad enough to care about their application, and

to have a friend or family member read it over for them before they send it in. I want them to care like that. I want them to be excited and enthusiastic for the chance, not just to cut and paste from the previous application, switch Perfect Plain in for (insert bar's name here), and fire it over. Want us to care about your application? You need to care about it yourself and value the job you're applying for.

2. **Anything that speaks to attitude and appreciation for a culture-empowered workplace.** People who display depth and understanding that they want a great place to work, and also show signs that they care enough to be part of creating a great place to work – that's music to my ears. We just received a head brewer application from a candidate with a decorated resume. But my favorite part of all was his cover letter that said that one of his goals was to bring a great attitude and cultivate a positive attitude among staff at work every day. That speaks to me as a culture-focused owner and moved him immediately to the top of my list.

3. **I *love* when people are passionate about things other than beer.** We have a florist on staff. We have female Air Force veteran who used to be a jet engine mechanic. We have someone who told us during an end-of-year review that he was happy working here, but was considering leaving the hospitality industry to become an insurance adjuster. To fuel his passion, we told him we would give him $250 to use for training or testing to chase that dream. We gave Chrissy, our resident bartender/florist, $250 to go to any training she would like to build her skills as a florist. I love people with varied backgrounds and passions. It brings depth, variety, and different perspectives to your staff.

Once I have that group of finalists, I sort them into A or B candidates. I want to start all A candidates in the process first, and I'll wait to vet those A candidates first before I start the process with the B candidates.

Make sure both you and the open position's direct report are involved in the decision of prioritizing the frontrunners. Your direct report has to deal with this person every day, so even if you think you already know which direction both of you would like to go, it's vital that the direct report feel involved in the process from the beginning. Make sure the direct supervisor has signed off on whatever finalist list you come up with.

For this chapter example, let's work under the assumption that I've got three strong candidates.

Step 1: The HR Interview

I always chuckle at this title, because for Perfect Plain, and probably the vast majority of breweries out there, the owner is *also* the HR department. Unfortunately, at our stage in life we don't have a Toby Flenderson we can utilize as our HR punching bag. (For the uninitiated, that's a reference to *The Office*.)

Preferably, this will be an in-person interview, but it can be handled over the phone for out-of-town candidates when it is not practical to have them in person.

The desired outcome of this first interview is *not* to vet their technical acumen. You have Step 2 for that. This is for culture and company fit only. This is your attempt to sign off on them as a representative of your company. Your line of questioning should be about culture and learning more about them as a person. You should be asking questions to get a feel for the type of person they are and get a glimpse of their employee values and their ability to be a strong teammate. You're looking for someone to become part of your family.

I'm a firm believer in behavioral-based questions. You may have heard of these, and a quick Google search can provide a multitude of examples to choose from. Some of my personal favorites:

- "Tell me about a time when you broke the rules because you thought it was the right thing to do."
- "What's the biggest mistake you've ever made at work?"
- "Tell me about a time you had a conflict with a coworker. What happened and how did you solve it, if at all?"

For each job, I have a custom set of 10–12 behavioral-based questions that I put into a graph like this where I can record a score from 1 to 5 for each answer. The questions shown are used in Step 3, the peer interview, but can be interchanged based on the desired outcomes of Steps 1 and 2.

INTERVIEW MATRIX TEMPLATE

Perfect Plain Brewing Company – Peer Interview

Position _____

Date: ___ / ___ / ___

Candidate _____

Interviewer _____

Core Competency (*such as, Communication, Customer Service, Teamwork*) Question (*Tell me about a time when you…*)	Weight 1–3	Score 1–5 5=Excellent 4=Very Good 3=Good 2=Fair 1=Poor	Comments/Notes:
1. Tell me about the best boss you ever had. Why did you like working for him or her?			
2. Think of a problem customer you had to deal with on your last job. Tell me what happened and how you handled it.			
3. Describe a time when you met someone in a work situation that seemed unapproachable. What did you do?			
4. Tell me about a time you worked on a team that accomplished excellent results. What were the main factors in the team's success?			

5. Have you heard the expression "roll with the punches"? What would be a situation in the past in which you had to do that?		
6. What questions do you have for us?		

RECOMMEND TO HIRE: (*Circle one*)   Yes   No

NOTES FROM MANAGER/PEER TEAM DISCUSSION:

_____

_____

In our example, I would hold interviews with all three candidates and score them accordingly. I'm not a firm believer of saying that if one person scores a 45 and another person scores a 44 that you must move the 45 on first. There could be nonscored factors you liked about the 44, such as professional dress, greeting, nonverbal persona, and attitude. However, this should help you quantify candidates who are clearly better or worse than others, and it also gives you a measurable metric to recall their strengths as a candidate, so you're not just relying on "feel" and trying to remember who answered which questions best.

From Step 1 to Step 2: The Key to Success

Once you interview your candidates in Step 1, you decide which candidates to move forward to Step 2, their direct report, for their technical interview. Listen up, because this is the key to the entire hiring process, and the hardest pill for owners and CEOs to swallow:

Once you have sent someone forward to Step 2, the decision is officially out of your hands. The decision will be made by the direct report and the peers. (You'll see how that works in a moment.)

What does that mean? It means you should never, ever, ever put someone through to Step 2 if you are not completely ready to hire them to your staff. You are showing the trust in your staff to make a sound decision for your company, but you can't blame them for picking someone that *you* put through to them as a viable candidate. Same goes for your direct report's recommendation from Step 2 to Step 3. If you aren't ready to hire that person in your mind that day, you absolutely cannot put them through.

This is what makes this process difficult, but it's also what makes it so powerful. How beautiful is it that you're going to be empowering the heart of your company, your staff, to have the ultimate say on who they get to work with? What a great way to show your trust and to create buy-in companywide.

Not to worry: if you have any hesitation whatsoever, you have options. Maybe after your three interviews, there's a clear one you like, but there's a second candidate you'd be okay with. But you like Candidate 1 much better. What do you do? You send Candidate 1 through the process first and see how they fare. You're not required to send both through at the same time. It's perfectly okay to regulate candidate selection based on preference. And you know what? If your favorite candidate can't get through all three steps, you go back to Candidate 2 and send them up.

Step 2: The Technical Interview

This interview is done in person with at least one direct report, and in the cases of larger companies it's perfectly fine to have an additional leader included who will be directly involved in this candidate's employment. I would not put a taproom manager in a technical interview for a cellar position, but you could have an assistant brewer and a head brewer in Step 2 for a cellar job.

In the case of brewery operations jobs, this is the interview where I like our brewing staff to have a sit-down interview, a brew day, a walk-through of equipment – anything your brewing staff sees fit to vet them from a technical perspective. Discuss what your litmus test is beforehand so you can prepare the candidate. I'm not suggesting that this step is limited to just an interview. Vet this person's skill set in as many ways needed to get your comfort level satisfied before sending them to Step 3, the peer interview.

I would still follow the same behavioral-based questions and score sheet you had in Step 1, but the questions are geared now more toward a technical perspective. You can begin the interview with more traditional questions about their experience or any questions you have based on what they listed in their resume:

- "Give an example of when you used logic to solve a problem."
- "Tell me about a time you had to be very strategic in order to meet all your top priorities."

What if I'm the owner AND the head brewer? It's okay for you to conduct both the Step 1 and Step 2 interviews. But for the sake of a proper filtering of candidates, I would keep the subject matter in the exact same format. While you may be tempted to hear about their favorite NEIPA or CIP best practices in the first interview, keep the sanctity of the procedure together. And it's perfectly all right to share with an applicant that this first interview is about culture, and if a second interview is needed, that will cover the more technical aspects of the position.

Step 3: The Peer Interview

This is the final step before making a hire. I consider it the most important.

Why? They've passed your test as a cultural fit. They've passed the technical test. But so, so many great things happen when you get a "yes" from your peer interview panel.

Your employees know that their decision is impactful and affects the future of the company. That's how you create a sense of ownership.

"WHO HIRED THAT GUY?" Ever heard that before?

All of a sudden, when employees make the final decision on hiring, they are automatically invested in the success of their new peer. Who hired them? THEY did. If this person doesn't get the training, we're all responsible. No just blaming the owner or the boss. We're all in this together. You'll see a noticeable change in the investment of a strong onboarding for your new staff member.

Second, you won't *believe* what some interviewees will tell a panel of peers that they won't tell the boss. It's like the good-cop, bad-cop mental phenomenon we see on TV shows all the time. Some candidates get comfortable with peers and forget they're still interviewing for a job.

It didn't happen with us, but one company who employs this hiring process once had a candidate admit to stealing money from the register during a peer interview. And during one of our interviews, someone told me he was available to work on Sundays. Then at the peer interview he said he was not available to work on Sundays. That would have put an unfair strain on the staff, and he did not get through.

I know it seems crazy, but staff will get much more out of a candidate than an owner or CEO ever will. They're prepared for the CEO, but they often let their guard down around peers.

How the Peer Interview Works:

Some companies actually go through a formal certification process for an employee to become a peer interviewer. While you may not go to that extreme, it is vital for the people included to understand the process. It's also important that you position this process as not just an obligation for your staff, but as a privilege to ultimately choose their coworkers.

Never put a low-performing or mediocre employee on the peer interview committee. This is a reward for your highest performers, and certainly you value the opinion of your top performers the most.

- If you include lesser performers or people who have been reprimanded for performance on this team, you not only risk this person tainting the result, but you send the message to your highest performers that their hard work gives them no more say than another employee who doesn't perform as well. Fairness of inclusion or rotating this with every employee for this group is not a requirement. If you adapt this process, it's smart to have a rollout of this new process with your entire staff. A good start would be to let them read this chapter of the book.
- It is important to have a conversation with your high performers where everyone gets to talk about what they see as vital in all new hires before you set your first peer interview.
- I like to have three people on my peer interview team. More than three means fewer questions for each person. Having only one or two people isn't a large enough subset of peers.
- I allow each member of the peer interview team to choose their own four questions – whatever speaks to them. They should compare before the interview begins.
- After the interview, the candidate leaves, and the peers vote on whether they recommend hiring.

I know some companies will do a majority-rules vote. I don't like that. If you rely on a majority, companies now have one "I told you so" employee on staff who voted against this new hire. I require unanimous approval to make a job offer.

Whew, that's involved, right? Sure. But it's worth it, I promise you. It's worth giving up some authority on hiring. It's worth being extra, extra sure that this person is a great fit for your company. This is a process that I personally help install at small businesses often, and I'll go more in depth on this at MicrobreweryHandbook.com.

This process will take longer than a single-interview hiring structure. You have more interviews to schedule, and naturally fewer people are going to get through all three rounds. That requires more candidates and more time. It requires patience, and to steal a line from

Alabama head coach Nick Saban and New England Patriots coach Bill Belichick, you have to "trust the process."

However, when analyzed accurately, it's a time saver. The idea behind being more selective about staff does all those great things: better culture, less turnover, and higher employee engagement, which leads to better customer service

Think about how much time you or your staff invests personally when you are short-staffed. Think about the overtime hours you are paying out as hires that are not vetted to this standard continue to move in and out of your company.

The Non-Negotiables of Three-Step Interviewing

- No friends of a candidate should be involved in any step of the process, especially in peer interviewing. As you can imagine, if I'm one of three peers on an interview panel, I would feel pressure to approve someone I knew was friends with a coworker when that person is sitting in the same interview as I am. You should keep as much bias out of the process as possible.

- I try to limit conversations about job applicants as they are handed off. It's perfectly natural for me to talk to my GM between Step 1 and Step 2 about how the first interview went. It's tempting to pour praise over that person to your GM – heck, I've done it myself – but I try to limit that to avoid influencing the GM's decision making or make them feel pressure to put someone through because I liked them.

- These three steps have to be followed religiously. And that entails sacrifices. It means if you are an owner or leader in the organization, you must not undercut the process or you will be undercutting the integrity of your hires. And that sends a message to your staff that their opinion only matters when you want it to, and that is not a message you want to convey.

Chapter 17

How to Have Happy Employees

Keep Them Engaged

WHEN YOU HAVE the leadership piece firmly in place as well as sound hiring processes, it's time to invest in the most important, valuable, expensive, and more unpredictable asset you have. People. Here are some tactical measures we have put in place to engage our Perfect Plain staff.

1. Onboarding, 30-Day, and 90-Day Conversations with All New Staff

More than a quarter of the American workforce leaves their respective jobs within the first 90 days of employment.

Think about your first day on the job. It's great! Everyone is nice! It's that honeymoon effect. You don't know what you don't know yet. Soon after, things change. You start to realize how much you don't know about your job. You may feel like you lack the skills to keep up. Quint Studer calls this "unconsciously incompetent" (as compared to "consciously competent"), or perhaps better known to us all as the "Oh shit!" moment.

This is why onboarding is important.

So often we hire someone new, then move them right into action with little concern about how they're doing. It makes all the difference if you have a strong onboarding plan that includes training – both on your culture and the job – and pairing up your new hire with a high-performing mentor or buddy to teach them the ropes.

One cool program with mentors works this way: A mentor gets $500 for the successful onboarding of an employee: $200 after the training is complete, and $300 more 365 days after the new hire started. That keeps the mentor invested and incentivized longer than a week to bring that new hire along. Might be worth trying with your team.

111

Our managers are required to have documented 30-day and 90-day chats with every single hire. (We try and be careful not to call these "reviews," but conversations. There are no grades to give them here.) You can see the sample forms here and download them at MicrobreweryHandbook.com.

30-Day Questions

Employee Name:
Role:
Leader Conducting Session:
Start Date:
Date of 30-Day Meeting:

Question	What Was Heard	Action Taken, Including Tokens of Appreciation, If any & Entering of Bright Ideas	Date Completed or Next Follow-Up
How do we compare with what we said during the interview process?			
What's working well?			
Have there been any individuals who have been helpful to you?			
Based on your prior work, what ideas for improvement do you have?			
Should I worry about losing you?			

Indicate overall Employee Satisfaction level on scale of 1–10: _____
  10=Very satisfied
  5=Somewhat satisfied, unsure whether right place for them
  1=Very dissatisfied, likely to leave

Now that this person has been in your department for 30 days, do you feel based on what you have seen so far, that they were a good hire?

Please rate on a scale of 1–10: _____

90-Day Questions

Employee Name:
Role:
Leader Conducting Session:
Start Date:
Date of 90-Day Meeting:

Question	What Was Heard	Action Taken, Including Tokens of Appreciation, If any & Entering of Bright Ideas	Date Completed or Next Follow-Up
How do we compare with what we said?			
What's working well?			
Have there been any individuals who have been helpful to you?			
Based on your prior work, what ideas for improvement do you have?			
Is there any reason that you feel this is not the right place for you?			
Do you know of anyone who would be a good fit for our organization?			
As your supervisor, how can I help you?			

Indicate overall Employee Satisfaction level on scale of 1–10: _____
   10=Very satisfied
   5=Somewhat satisfied, unsure whether right place for them
   1=Very dissatisfied, likely to leave
Now that this person has been in your department for 90 days, do you feel based on what you have seen so far, that this is a good hire?

Please rate on a scale of 1–10: _____

The key outcome here is that your new employees have a dedicated time to talk about what's going well and any questions they have. Saying "How's it going?" as you breeze past them in the taproom isn't an effective way to check on new staff. What do you expect them to say? They are going to say things are going well, even if they aren't. Carving out this dedicated time is vital.

You also find out if you have all the tools your employees need to do their job, another thing that is often overlooked without a specific sit-down conversation.

We've learned many important things that we've ended up implementing companywide through these meetings.

Midyear and End-of-Year Conversations

Much like 30- and 90-day conversations, these are pulse checks, but this time on all managers and staff. This means twice a year you're taking the time to listen, learn, and react.

We send these forms out to all staff in advance, and they are required to fill them out and return them to their direct supervisor at least 24 hours before their meeting.

We call these "conversations," not reviews. There is no grade. This lowers anxiety with staff. It's a conversation about what's going well. The first question on the end of year, about accomplishments, always gets the meeting off on the right foot. Most times, neither the employee nor the leader has truly sat down to appreciate all that was accomplished in the previous year. It's a time to be grateful and celebrate.

It is also a chance for the organization to reprioritize to staff what's important that next year. You'll see some similar questions like "Do we have to worry about losing you?"

I would say that 99 percent of the time, these check-ins have the leader and employee both feeling good about themselves, their jobs, and the company. And likely, there's some great adjustments made for the next six months or year that would never have happened without these meetings.

Wins all around.

Midyear and end-of-year conversation forms can be found at Microbreweryhandbook.com.

Dogfish Head CEO Sam Calagione on his approach to communication with leadership and direct reports

Leaders do mandated one-on-ones with direct reports through an HR software portal hub called Halogen. It kind of manages an expectation that all leaders meet with each of their reports one on one monthly so that they're really proactively communicating what direction they and the company are going in and allowing the folks who report to them an equal opportunity to ask questions and have input. Because in small companies, it's easy to get in trouble by saying, "We all know what we're doing. We're too busy to meet. Let's just keep doing what we're doing. I trust you. You trust me." Without regular check-ins, it's too easy to start going off of paths and have resentment or confusion. So, that very regular, scheduled communication, while it might sound like a hassle in corporate to say we're going to sit down one on one every month, it usually pays dividends for keeping the relationships and overall communication of the company healthy.

Employee Engagement Survey

We conduct an employee engagement survey each January. This should be a requirement for any brewery, from 3 employees to 3,000.

The submissions are completely anonymous. Each question is rated on a 1-to-5 scale. There are organizations like not-for-profit Studer Community Institute in Pensacola that conducts these with smaller companies, and on the larger scale, Chris Reilly with Sperduto and Associates. Both are excellent at conducting and analyzing the data.

With 10 employees, I feel comfortable conducting my own, and these are the questions I use. As we grow, I will probably grow the survey, then eventually outsource it. But if you can start with asking your staff these questions on a 1-to-5 scale, then see where you are strongest and where you are weakest, that will prescribe a nice starting plan for owners and leaders to improve your overall employee engagement.

1. I feel proud when I tell people where I work.
2. Employees are fully committed to the success of the organization.
3. I recommend this as a good place to work.
4. I have confidence in the abilities of my leader.
5. My leader cares about me as a person.
6. My leader treats people fairly.
7. My leader recognizes results and accomplishments.
8. My leader takes corrective action when necessary.
9. The organization employs people with whom I like to work.
10. My coworkers and I share a strong work ethic.
11. Many of my coworkers are performing at an acceptable level or better.
12. I feel connected to my coworkers.
13. The work I do is meaningful.
14. When at work, I fully immerse myself in my job.
15. Employees are treated fairly.
16. This is a comfortable environment in which to work.
17. I am satisfied with my working conditions.
18. I have a clear understanding of what is expected of me in my work.
19. I receive the support needed to accomplish my work objectives.
20. I put more effort into my job than is required.
21. I am recognized for doing things well.
22. Credit in my organization goes to those who deserve it.
23. My coworkers go out of their way to help customers.
24. The organization is dedicated to the satisfaction of its customers.
25. Good customer service is rewarded by leaders.
26. "Customers come first" is accurate.
27. The organization is ethical in its treatment of employees.

28. The organization is ethical in its treatment of customers.
29. The organization's leaders model ethical behavior.
30. I feel safe reporting a possible ethics breach to appropriate leader(s) or HR.
31. The organization takes appropriate action when possible ethics breaches are reported.
32. I am encouraged by the direction of the organization.
33. The organization makes adjustments to stay competitive in the industry.
34. My overall level of satisfaction is:

One large benefit is that you can sometimes diagnose and address potential issues that are lurking in your business, especially the silent ones that can erode your employee engagement.

Recently a healthcare equipment company conducted a large-scale survey with its employees for the first time. The lowest scored result was about compensation, specifically with salary and benefits. This surprised leadership. They paid more than competitively, what's the problem?.

This company had two offices, one in Florida and one in Ohio. Turns out that when all employees signed up for their benefits each year, it would show both healthcare plans, one for Florida and one for Ohio. The Florida plan was always cheaper. This was not because the company was offering a better deal to Florida employees; there were certain state rules that caused the Ohio plan to be slightly more expensive for the exact same benefits. All the company needed to do was explain this point, they just didn't realize it had caused an issue.

Once diagnosed, it was an easy discussion with staff. They understood. But without the employee engagement survey, that point would have festered in the out-of-state office, and assumptions would have been made that they aren't treated as well as the Florida employees. The water cooler talk could have gotten away from them and led to bigger culture problems.

To steal another hospital analogy, you can't treat what you don't diagnose. In our 2019 survey, while our survey results were strong – our lowest-scoring category was a 4.3 – we realized that the common themes among our lowest-scoring items all circled around reward and recognition. We realized we weren't doing a good enough job rounding and managing up our staff.

Standards of Behavior

We have created standards of behavior that outline our expectations for every one of our employees.

This is our six-page document that we require all interviewees – not employees, but interviewees – to sign before they get their first interview at Perfect Plain. Our feeling is that if you are unwilling to live to these standards, there's really no reason to waste our time or the candidate's time. Refer to our Standards of Behavior form in Appendix 3.

Each year, we open up these standards for discussion company wide, make any changes or additions that we agree on, and we ask them to re-sign the standards annually. It keeps everyone involved in helping shape the culture of our company and also keeps them top of mind. Many companies have standards of behavior, but often employees only sign them during the human resources/onboarding process and then never look at them again. This way they stay fresh, updated, and cognizant of the expectations of all employees.

Training and development. How may dollars do you set aside in your budget each year for training and development for your staff? You may spend money, but do you have a strategy behind those dollars?

All brewing staff as well as our front-of-house managers are allotted dollars annually in their employee agreement to spend and help make decisions on their own skill development during the year. If they think, say, Craft Brewers Conference is a way they want to use some of those dollars, great. If a trip to New England to learn and benchmark brewers there is a possibility, we take a look at that too. While all development is approved by ownership, we enable our staffers to take part in their own development. We believe that leads to stronger use of dollars instead of being told to go somewhere.

Part of the trade-off for that open selection of external skill development is that we ask each person to report back on what they learned, maybe 1–2 pages that we can keep on file, then also come up with 2–3 action items based on the experience. If we thought the training would be good and it turned out to be a bust, that's okay. We ask the employee to report that "whiff" back to us so we at least know it's not worth going to the next time.

Communicate openly about company goings on. Employees care about getting updates way more than you think. You may think that new tank or news about a new restaurant opening next door has nothing to do with your bartending staff. But it does. Most high-performing staffs like knowing what's going on in the organization, even if it doesn't affect them directly. And remember, the more included they feel, the more loyal they are to you and your company.

Learn the personalities of your staff. Do some personality tests and have fun with it during a monthly staff meeting. Maybe make up a quiz and say, "Who is the most like this?" and give a prize to the staff members who knew their coworkers best. We use *Management by Strengths (MBS)*, but there are so many behavioral/personality tests out there.

The biggest value I've gotten out of this as an owner is knowing more about each individual. Let's say I have a critique on something. I know that because of their differing personalities, the way I approach BB, my events and marketing manager, is completely different than how I approach Nate, our general manager. Nothing right or wrong with either person, but they digest and compute "bad news" differently. It's valuable to know that ahead of time instead of hurting feelings or getting upset because you don't understand how the receiver's mind works.

Chapter 18

Common Barriers to a Strong Company Culture

WHAT GETS IN the way of building a strong culture? There are countless resources online for how to build a strong company culture, but I've highlighted some rules and tactics here that can trip up your quest to create a great place to work.

As the owner, head brewer, or both, whether you like it or not, you set the tone for your entire company. How you act, how you treat people, and how much you pay attention to the little things will spread through the organization.

I like having open conversations with my staff about these barriers because they are prevalent, and I want to keep employees aware of these traps to prevent falling in. And if I hold our leadership staff accountable in these areas, the expectation is that those leaders will do the same with the operations staff.

We/They

I'd be willing to bet you this is happening at your organization right now. In fact, there's a good chance *you* are doing it as the owner or manager right now, and you don't even know the negative impact it has. It's very easy to fall prey to this, and at one time or another we all do it.

It's called *we/they*. I learned this from Quint, and even though I still make this mistake time to time, I'm glad I'm aware of it so I can try to minimize it.

We/they is when an owner, manager, or employee, in essence, takes the wins as their own and gives away the losses by blaming/rationalizing those on someone else, most commonly the owner, manager, or company itself.

Here's an example: Joe, an employee, is asking Nate, the manager, for time off on late notice.

Joe: Hey Nate, I was wondering, is there any way I can have next week off to visit my family?

At this point, you know that two other employees have been granted time off next week, and requested it in advance, well before Joe did. But here's the dilemma and the cause for *we/they:* No one wants to be the bad guy, especially when Joe tells us he's going to see family. This avoidance of being the boss, not the friend, may be the most common cause of we/they. Nate, the manager, has a choice. As the manger, if it's not possible to accommodate Joe, he should explain to Joe that he cannot give him that time off he requested because it's not available and we'll try and accommodate the next time.

Unfortunately, what often happens is a manager doesn't want to own "the loss." Instead, the manager says, *"Let me go ask D.C., the owner."*

This is a big mistake. Why?

First, Nate has now mttessaged to Joe that he's *not* in charge. He has undercut his own authority in the organization, and he's telling his direct reports that if they truly want something done, they might as well skip him and go ask the owner since he or she makes all the decisions.

So, we play out our scenario: Nate asks D.C., and D.C. says no, it's against company policy. Joe can't be given the time off. How does Nate message this news to Joe? This is where the we/they happens.

Nate: "Well I talked to D.C., and it looks like he can't give you that time off."

So Nate has officially saddled the owner with the loss to save his own goodwill with that employee.

This can erode an employee's engagement with the company over time. Interestingly enough, you can actually sniff out *we/they* in your organization if you are doing an annual employee engagement survey (see Chapter 17). How can you tell? If your employees *love* their direct manager, but they rate the overall organization significantly lower, you can rest assured you have a manager who is not positioning the company well.

Now let's say our company figured out a way to still get Joe his vacation time despite the late notice. How Nate messages good news is just as important. The natural tendency is to "take the win," as in

Nate saying, *"Don't worry Joe, I've taken care of it for you. I pulled some strings, You're all good."* The reality might be that the owner or the organization is bending its own rules to accommodate, and if that's the case, it's a great situation for that manager not only to get the win of delivering the good news to Joe, but also position the company well by saying something like, "Although this is company policy, I've discussed it with leadership, and since you've been working so hard these past few weeks we all agreed that we wanted to make an exception. Thank you for being a part of our team and giving us great effort lately."

That's how a manager positions his company well – getting goodwill directly and positioning it well with the company.

This happens most commonly with enforcing company policies, granting favors or benefits to employees, and the like. While I believe no organization in the world is perfect at eliminating *we/they*, this is a very important topic to bring up with brewery management and to practice how to communicate in a way that's fair to them and the organization.

Difficult Conversations and Lack of Documentation

This is another weak point for so many businesses, including Perfect Plain. We're talking about this constantly as a point of improvement.

We've all had those days. One employee is getting on our nerves because they didn't close down the taproom correctly *again!* How often do we as managers complain about certain employees without actually addressing this issue directly with the employee?

I think I've annoyed my managers about this to the point where they don't complain about these minor issues much anymore unless they can say they've taken some level of action.

Perhaps one of our managers makes an off-handed comment during a meeting about an employee not following the closing procedures. Instead of being tempted to join in on this, I immediately ask the complaining manager, "Have you spoken with the employee about this?" I expect that if you are bringing it up, at a minimum this should have been done already. If it's something more serious or something happening consistently, I'll ask if the manager has documented it with the employee.

Point is, I challenge my leadership to manage and develop our employees. If Joe the bartender isn't closing right, are we are saying nothing, not coaching, and then just complaining when it's only leadership in the room? If that's the case, I see that as the manager's fault, not the employee's.

No matter the industry, violations of rules at work are grossly underdocumented. I get it. You feel like a stickler doing it, and it's not a fun conversation to have. So, what do we do? We complain about it in a managers' meeting, then move on and forget about it until the next time.

But what if it becomes a recurring issue? What if you're ready to fire an employee, and they ask what they did wrong? Are you going to open an empty employee folder with no complaints and all these great annual reviews because you were too scared to mention any need for improvement?

I highly recommend two of Quint Studer's books, *Results that Last* and *Hardwiring Excellence,* for a deeper dive on employee culture and how to construct it. Much of what we implement at Perfect Plain is derived – and modified for our industry – from these books. Chapter 1 of *Results that Last* is an excellent resource on how to handle and message difficult conversations effectively.

Here's one more example: Our local Double-A baseball team, the Pensacola Blue Wahoos, was having an issue with complaints about its seasonal employees (food service, ushers, etc.) working one season, then being denied a job the next year and having no idea why.

You can predict what was happening. Low-performing employees' violations weren't being documented, and so instead of dealing with the documentation and/or difficult conversations of suspending or firing the employee, senior management would avoid addressing it and just "sweat out" the remainder of the season with this person on staff, then not invite them back the next year. Problem solved, right?

Wrong. It left these low-performing employees completely unaware of why they weren't brought back, which meant that person would be going into the community bad-mouthing the organization to friends and family, saying he or she was treated unfairly.

The team came up with a creative solution to curb this. A policy was put in place that if *any* seasonal employee was still on staff at the end of the season, they were an automatic rehire the next year. No questions asked.

Managers have a duty to have difficult conversations with employees sometimes, including developmental conversations. Maybe it's about shoring up beer knowledge, or moving faster behind the bar, or tactfully breaking out of bar conversations with guests when the taproom is busy. Make sure you message to your leadership not to take a reactive approach to managing your employees. They need to be proactive in teaching the best practices, and proactive in removing low-performing employees.

One exercise is to ask that once a month each of your managers do a developmental session, working on something with a specific direct report, then report that back to your leadership team.

Tip: Let's say that you want to start creating more accountability with staff, but since you haven't been doing it for a long time – or ever – it would be "out of the blue" or awkward to just pick a random day and start.

Here's a sample staff-wide explanatory paragraph included in an e-mail to their direct reports that helps reshuffle the deck and reopen that door. (This follows an introduction and a positive start to the e-mail, such as "We had a great week/event last week," etc.)

Part of the mission of our company is to create a great place to work, and one important way to do that is to have a strong commitment to our coworkers. Recently, some minor things have been missed or forgotten by many staff, if not all, during day-to-day operations, and I've let you down by not being more vocal about it. In these cases, they were all innocent omissions or slipups, but my unwillingness to speak up has made it unfair to the employees who have been following the rules perfectly and it is sending the message that our standard operating procedures and rules can or cannot be followed, depending on the person. I know you all know that's not the case, and your understanding of our rules is what makes you valuable employees.

This week I'll do a better job of making sure I'm pointing out missteps. It's not to discourage you or to say you aren't doing great work for us. When minor slipups are mentioned, please don't take it personally. We are all committed to having a great workplace and a great work environment, and without accountability in place I haven't lived up to the standard I'm putting on you all. I apologize, and please feel free to reach out to me with any questions.

What has your supervisor done? They've taken responsibility, they have not placed blame on the employee for any mistakes, and they've in essence opened the door for your employees to expect more accountability going forward without creating fear of anger or retaliation.

What You Permit, You Promote

This is simple. Along the lines of the previous tip, if you are going to allow one employee to have a consistent bad attitude when they come to work, or that one employee always gets their drinks for free against company policy, you may as well have a billboard in your workroom that says to the entire organization, "I don't care about enforcing any rules here. Do whatever you'd like."

This means the owner, too. If I walk into the Perfect Plain taproom and ignore a pile of trash on the ground, I'm letting my staff know it's okay for them to do that, too. When I see the garbage overflowing on a Saturday when I'm just hanging out at the taproom with friends, I jump up and take it out. Perhaps it makes the staff uncomfortable to see the owner doing that. That's all right. It demonstrates the expectation that we're all team players here in making this place successful, owner included. And in our case, we have such a great staff, it could be super busy on a Saturday and they just haven't gotten to it. That's perfectly okay; I don't judge a full trash can (every now and then) as a lack of effort. However, when you show that it's important to you as the owner, it will naturally cascade and become important to your staff.

How can you expect your employees to treat your brewery like it's their own if you don't treat it like it's your own? The point here is to know that your staff is watching you and your leaders at all times, and they get their cues off of that. Things you don't mention or seem to care about will get pushed to the back burner, while things you are on top of will become their top priority. Know that and act accordingly.

Eliminate Ambiguity

This is a big one for me. How many meetings have you been in where you discuss something for 30 minutes, then you come back the next week and realize no progress was made? It happens all the time.

What should have happened is you tap a point person for that project. They are the ones accountable for making this project go. Often we don't take the extra time to eliminate the ambiguity of a situation. Who owns this? Who is responsible for this? Who will check back up and make sure this is done?

I'm inherently not good at structure – every Myers-Briggs or Management By Strengths personality test tells me that. I'm nimble, I like to brainstorm, and I'm a great problem solver, and I'm motivated by people and how decisions affect people. I'm a people person. But I need people around me to bring that structure to make sure we are following up on things. That's why eliminating ambiguity is a must for me.

(An important side note: As mentioned earlier in the book, it's also valuable to have all your staff take a personality test if you can afford to so you know how best to communicate with them. How they hear your communication may be different than you think, so this is another great way to eliminate ambiguity.)

Multiple studies have shown that about 80 percent of failure can be attributed to ambiguity.

Lack of Communication

Can you tell me the last time you had an employee come up to you and say, "Wow, I get exactly the right number of e-mails! Not too many, not too few, it's just perfect."

We communicate a lot at Perfect Plain. More than your average bar or brewery. I'm a talker by nature – I think my staff would nod their heads to this assessment – and maybe that's projected here, but I believe that it's better to overcommunicate than undercommunicate. We bring this up with staff well before they are hired so it's fully expected.

If employees complain that they get too many e-mails, I often say that this is much better than the alternative of not getting enough information. Mistakes and oversights happen without communication.

Again, our taproom bartenders are making about $30 to $35 per hour. I feel like a few extra e-mails per week can be handled. By the way, I'd venture to guess that some of these communications may be informing them about new beers on draft that, when read and cascaded to our customers, can lead to more tips. Don't be afraid to position communication that way.

Chapter 19

Employee Engagement Q&A: Quint Studer

D.C. Reeves: If someone reads about you in this book and the work you've done with major hospital systems, they may make the case that, "Hey, I have five or six employees, why does this matter to me?"

Why should a small company follow some of the structure behind your beliefs about employee engagement – 30- and 90-day conversations, transparency, onboarding, and a three-step hiring process?

Quint Studer: Actually, the smaller you are, the more vital it is. For example, one of the things I used to say is "If you have five employees and you have one problem employee, 20% of your employees are problem employees." So, they will actually impact you more than if you had five problem employees out of 1,000 employees. So the smaller you are, the more important it is to do these things.

When I started my own small company, Studer Group, we had eight employees. Even at that time, I hired an outside company to come in and do an employee engagement survey with just those eight. The survey company said they had never done one this small, and I said "Well, I want to do it right now because I don't know if we'll get bigger if we don't do it right."

One of the biggest things I see with small businesses is they think, "I'll do it when I get bigger." The problem is, you might not get bigger if you don't do it, because early on you are laying the foundation. Because your third employee is going to learn from your first employee, your eighth employee is going to learn from your first seven employees. So you are creating the foundation of your culture.

To build a home on Pensacola Beach – and most beaches – you have to put in pilings, and if you don't put your pilings in deep enough, eventually that house won't last. But here's the thing – you don't *have* to put them in deep, and if you're in a real hurry to build you just put them in a little bit, put the house up there, and hope to gosh everything works out okay. But a smart builder makes that foundation sound for years to come.

In small business with your first employees, the processes you're putting in place are your pilings, and if you don't put them in right, the company won't grow right.

DC: So let's say I start a business, and in most cases a small, taproom-only business is going to have a lot of multitasking, the same employee wearing a lot of hats. It's quite easy to rationalize and say, "Do I have time to conduct these four conversations each year? I don't have time to do these things. I don't have the resources to do that."

So, let's tie this effort of employee engagement to an outcome for small business. What makes this worth my time in the early phases?

QS: With hospital CEOs, sometimes I found myself having to look at it the opposite way: *Let's say we don't do these things.* For example, when I was president of a hospital, we were really focusing on patient experience. The CEO visited me and said, "Wow, Quint, you spent a lot of time on this patient experience stuff. Doesn't that take lot of time?"

I said, "A lot less time than dealing with bad patient experiences."

You get a person who is unhappy, that's going to eat you alive. You're dealing with an unhappy employee, it's going to eat you alive. So, think about all the hours and time you spent because you don't do those things. I have found that that's the best way to get people to look at both sides. Don't just look at the time it takes to execute it. Add up all of that time and see how much it costs you not to do it.

Here's the outcome: You're going to have better retention of employees. If you have better retention of employees, you're going to have better retention of clients. Particularly in a craft beer setting, people like familiarity, people want to come in and have people recognize them. They're going to want an experience. When you look at craft beer, in my mind, the days of being first to market are either getting slim or are gone completely.

Many people start a company following their passion. My wife loves coffee and olive oil, so what did she start? A coffee and olive oil store. I liked changing cultures in healthcare. I didn't start a software company, I didn't start a revenue cycle company, which are really popular in healthcare. I started to improve employee engagement and patient experience because that's what I was passionate about.

The challenge then to grow my own company was that I still had to learn revenue. I still had to learn software, the things I didn't know much about. I think in craft beer, if you are not careful you get hung up on "I love creating the beer, I love creating the name," and you think that if you do that well, the business is going to take care of itself. And it won't. Or another mistaken approach: "I'm going to have this great building, it's going to be cooler than heck." It will get people there the first time, but unless you're creating that experience, which is programming it, fun, familiar, you're basically in my mind creating a community center that happens to also have beer.

DC: You go around the country and talk with small business owners in different cities. What are the two biggest pitfalls with small businesses that you see?

QS: First, assuming you communicated. A leader or owner says, "Well I talk to people a lot." Then the company does its first employee engagement survey, and one of the biggest complaints is "I don't know what's going on."

It's about taking time to say to your employees, "What do you want to know? When do you want to know it? How do you want to know it?" I think that's number one; just because you're talking a lot doesn't mean you're actually communicating. I think you have to have that intentional communication. Like, "Today I'm going to ask, 'Do you have the tools and equipment to do the job?'"

Same thing with clients or customers. "How is everything today? Did you get the right service? Is the taste what you expected? Gee, have you ever been to other craft breweries? Tell us some things you've seen other places you think we could do to be better."

Now if I go to a small business owner and ask them if they talk to their customers, they say, "Oh, yea, all the time!" But ask yourself: What do you learn from them? Think about that. People who come into a craft brewery have probably been to another one in their life-time. What have they seen that you could do here? Ask, "Hey, why do you like coming here? What are we offering?" Then you find out that somebody might like something you're thinking of getting rid of. So, I think it is that intentional conversation; we assume we've covered it because we've talked about it, and I think that's the big-gest misstep with a small company.

Number two is lack of clarity. Employees say, "We want to have a great place to work." Let's talk about standards of behavior. Let's talk about standards of performance. For example, if there's a dress code for employees and the chef comes out wearing a baseball cap turned on backwards, is that what you want? Or is it not what you want? When you're a small business, you may not take time when you should to let the employees create these standards as a team. Here's the type of culture we want to live, and here are the rules and standards of behavior to do that.

Small businesses all think they have standards of behavior but they're not documented, they're not written down, and they're not understood. That's why the owner gets burned out, because they feel they've got to be there all the time. If you have good standard operating procedures, good standards of behavior, everybody under-stands. I think that's probably the biggest mistake, assuming you don't have to either because you're there all the time, you assume everybody knows it, or you assume you're already doing it.

DC: One of the most difficult things to handle across any business at any size is the accountability factor, especially in a small busi-ness where you tend to know all your employees really well and you tend to see them more. How important is accountability and documentation, even in small settings?

QS: You have to ask yourself before you start a business: Can I fire a friend or a relative? If you can't, you're not going to have a great company, because those are the things that usually do people in. I started it with a buddy I went to college with, I'm hiring my brother or sister, something like that. That's okay, but if you're not willing to make those tough decisions, it can do you in.

I think that accountability piece, that's why the standards, the certain measurements come into play, because if you don't take action on those people then everybody is going to say, "As long as I work a little better than that, I'm okay."

And the other thing that's pretty interesting is that if you ask managers – and I can ask 100 managers – "Are you fair?" they're going to say, "Yes! I have some challenges, but the one thing I am is fair."

Then I'll ask about performance management and we'll ask the employees, "Is the boss fair?" and many employees will say "No." Then the manager is stunned. "Well, I pay the same benefits, I look at the schedule, I look at salary, I manage tips right, I manage work-load right, so what are they talking about – I am fair!"

The disconnect is that employees judge fairness on how you hold coworkers accountable, and that is their one data point. The other stuff they assume. Their data point is "How come Suzie gets to do this, and Bob and I don't? And you said you were going to hold every-body accountable, so how come Larry's now not shown up twice or left early and but he's still here?"

Once you start losing accountability, it's a corrosive threat that begins rusting the organization. I think the biggest mistake I see with small business owners is that of course they surround people early on with relatives and friends. That's okay if you can say to yourself, "I can fire a relative or friend."

DC: One thing that I've learned from you that's a drastically different mindset than most first-time business owners are used to is transparency with a company's financials. For people starting a first business who aren't familiar with the value, that suggestion might seem crazy. Explain why you think that financial transparency is not only important but is also actually a value to the owner or the company.

QS: For small businesses employees, just look at revenue. They have no idea there is debt, they have no idea there are taxes, they have no idea there is cost of goods. Employees just look at the end of the day: "We've had a $4,000 Saturday night. . . we've had a $1,200 Tuesday night," and they assume that somebody is getting rich on these things. And they really aren't, but I also think we want to create ownership, and I usually explain to CEOs the difference between an owner and a renter.

The sense of ownership story I tell is about me going to a fast-casual restaurant right before closing time. I was hungry, and this place was supposed to be open until 9 p.m. I was so excited, I drove there, it was like 8:45. I look and they're cleaning and they're putting the stools on top of the tables. I'm knocking and they're acting like I'm not there. Those are not the owners. The owner would have let me in. The owner would not have been doing that.

So, how do you get ownership from your entire staff? Well you get ownership; owners hire, so that's why you let your employees hire. It's why the three-tier hiring process allows employees ultimately to pick their colleagues. That's ownership. Owners also know the financials. I have found from big companies to little, if people know the financials, they get it.

My company, Studer Group, was very profitable. People did not worry if it was profitable and if I was making money as long as my compensation to them was fair. They know they're not expecting unrealistic compensation, but it also helps them. When I was a hospital CEO, we noticed that the IV tubing was very expensive, and we had nurses using more tubing than they needed because they didn't know the cost. Once they saw the cost, they started using the right amount of tubing.

If you don't give people the information, they're not going to make good decisions, particularly when you connect ownership to job security, getting the equipment they need, getting the right work environment they need. Everybody is always scared of transparency. But transparency equals accountability. Transparency is like breaking through the sound barrier. You're really afraid of it, you're shaking a little bit, then it goes out there and it's like, "Hmm, it's not as bad as I thought."

I had an employee come up to me one time and say, "I really like looking at the financials; it gives me a good idea of if I'm going to get overtime or not." I am just a huge believer in sharing financials. We share them with all our companies. Also, particularly in small businesses, people just assume there is more profit than there is, and the boss is making a zillion dollars.

I knew a guy who owned a small business. He was working another job on the side, yet his employees thought he was making a lot of money. He hadn't even taken a dime out of it in one year. I had him share that fact, and it dramatically changed the whole organization. They had no idea that he wasn't even taking any money out of there. And here they're thinking because he's driving a big truck, he's rich.

DC: At the healthcare level, you are often dealing with life and death, making negative customer interactions exponentially more difficult, more volatile, more anxiety ridden than what you may find at a brewery. What is your best advice when employees are dealing with a customer complaint?

QS: I think you have to not expect them to come to you; you've got to go to them. And I think it starts with empathy. You can talk about listening, but it's really empathy. So, they're disappointed, they're discouraged, they're angry, they're upset, something's wrong. And I think we get caught up in "Who's right?" That's not going to get you anywhere.

It's showing empathy. "I'm sorry you're frustrated, sorry you're upset, sorry it disappointed you." Then after listening, you quickly move into the key question: "What can I do to make this right?"

I find most of the time it's so much simpler to make it right than we think. Those complaining customers are usually not asking for anything extravagant. Is there anything I can do to make this right? Anything I can do right now to help you feel better about this? In bars, breweries, and restaurants, a free beer or coupon can be a very accessible and manageable fix.

And 99 percent of the time it's resolved when handled this way, and I love the fact that over the years research shows if you have a person with a problem, then you resolve it, they're actually *more* loyal to your company than somebody that did not have a problem in the first place. I used to joke that hotels should intentionally have one burned-out light bulb next to the bed and be standing out in the hallway with a working light bulb. So, the second they get the call from the guest about the broken lamp, they knock on the door, replace the light bulb in seconds, and build customer loyalty stronger than ever.

So I would say that empathy is the key. Try to say, "I understand, I'm disappointed. I'm sorry we let you down, you feel let down, what can I do to make this right, right now?"

And then you can either say, "I can do it," or "I can't do it." That's assuming, of course, that the person is not intoxicated. Now if you're dealing with someone who's out of control, then the question is, how do you get them out of the situation?

"Can you come with me here?" and walk them to a more secluded area of the taproom. We want to fix complaints, but sometimes you also have to have a fine line that you're not going to let somebody abuse somebody.

You're not going to let somebody go overboard. I mean, believe it or not, even in healthcare you run into people where you have to draw the line. Or sometimes there might be a physician who gets upset with a staff member.

And you have to say, "We just won't allow that. We won't tolerate that here."

DC: One thing that might be a new concept in craft beer that would benefit everybody is "rounding." Again, it's something that started in healthcare. How would you suggest a manager or owner or both focus on rounding and why is it important?

QS: One of the biggest misses I find in hospitality is what I call the "fast round" or "fast connections." Rounding comes from the concept of doctors making the rounds on patients, meaning that they're checking up to see how the patients are doing. I'm checking up to see if the prescription or procedure is now working, and if it's not working, what more do I need to do, what questions they need to be answered, and what is the treatment plan. The desired outcome is to find out if what you're doing is working.

This would work the same in craft beer. And it can also have similar "fast rounding" mistakes in a taproom setting.

Rounding is not just saying, "How are you? Everything okay today?" And I find when I go to any hospitality setting, employees are thinking almost like, "I just want to check the box . . . I've rounded today."

Everybody reading this book has been to a restaurant where a manager comes out and says, "Everything okay? How is everything?" And what are you almost always going to hear? "Fine."

Many of us have actually paid our tab and made a decision that we're never coming back to the place. And nevertheless, when the waiter, bartender, or manager asks, "How was everything?" we'll probably say "fine," pay, and walk out. But we are never coming back.

Employees are hesitant to round effectively because it's a little more hassle. Or they may hear something negative and they don't feel they want to create their own "problem." I think when you round effectively you want a mix of general rounding and some specific rounding. In more general rounding it would be something like:

- "What is important to you at Perfect Plain?"
- "Did you find the beer style you were looking for?"
- "Do we have the selection that you thought we would have?"
- "Was the service or the responsiveness what you expected?"

You pick: It's a menu. Choose about 10 questions to train your staff on. The staff doesn't have to ask them every day, but you've got to have that rotation. You can be more specific, too. "Have you used the restrooms? Were they up to your standards?

You haven't? Well you know what, if you do, we really want to make sure our restaurants are clean. If for some reason you don't think they are up to par, let me know." You're almost trying to make them your teammate in running the business. Customers want to feel good and believe they have input. I just think that's such a missing thing. "We like to compliment our staff. Are there any employees whom you'd like us to make sure we say good job to?"

You see the point. If I just go through and say, "Is everything fine?" I miss the opportunity either to reward and recognize someone or to coach someone. I think that's what rounding is: opportunities to get better or to reward the people who are doing a good job.

DC: And how about rounding on employees, more of the internal leader rounding on his or her employees. What are some guiding principles for that?

QS: If you look at research, it almost says that you should do this once every seven days with an employee. But you've got to rotate so you have to figure out what type to employ. The number one reason a person leaves their job is "I don't like my boss."

For some employees, you've got to know what's important to them. So if they have children, know their names and their hobbies. My assistant Barbara Scott has two boys, Cordson and Charles, and Cordson is taking swimming lessons right now. I can ask her how he's doing at swimming.

That will go a long way.

If you only have time for one question with an employee, it is this: "Do you have what you need to do your job today?" They're either going to say yes or no. The majority of the time they're going to say yes.

The problem is that because we don't play offense and we play defense, for three weeks your staff can have everything they need. But you come in on Tuesday and they say, "We're out of ice again." So by playing offense, you're drilling down. Then that next question is: "Hey, are there any employees you think I should recognize today?"

If you're a manager and owner, you're not going to see everything. You're not going to be there certain shifts. You're not going to see when certain things happen. So you want to be able to go in there and say, "Wow, we were really busy last night, and Susie came out from being cut earlier in the night and started clearing off tables for us and we really appreciate that."

You want to round for these things with staff, to show you care about them genuinely, do they have what they need to do the job and are you getting the communication you need.

One last thing on employee rounding, particularly with people who came from other places, you should ask this question: "Now that you've been here a while, are there things that you've seen done at other breweries that you think if we did them, we would be better?"

Breweries spend lots of time trying to find best practices. Heck, we'll go on a trip to a conference to find best practices. And when a best practice walks into our business, we avoid it.

Employees have normally been told, "Hey, don't tell how you used to do it there, because you're not there anymore." So, an employee has been trained to think, "Hey, when you go to this new place, don't talk about your old job."

So we've got to make it okay by saying, "Hey D.C., you just came from this brewery. I know they did a lot of great things. Now that you've been here a while, what are some things that they're doing?" You constantly want to maximize the intellectual capital of your workforce. And then they feel better about themselves, too.

Part IV

Creating an Incredible Customer Experience

WE CAN ALL name that brewery or restaurant we've been to where we love the product, but the service flat out stinks.

And we've heard the stories or seen the news clips of a company's indifference to its customers sometimes being romanticized as "part of the experience." Perhaps more than in other industries, some breweries have a knack for this.

However, studies show that paying no mind to your customer experience is a recipe for failure. (Yes, even if you make great beer.)

Focusing some time on that experience – from operations to customer service to programming your taproom – can make a world of difference. This is why creating incredible customer experiences - not just in beer quality, but in so many other facets - is part of Perfect Plain's mission statement. Let's discuss how to up your game for your guests.

Chapter 20
Customer Service Tips

Among the hustle and bustle of construction, when opening or growing a business some simple yet important training can fall through the cracks. This is why an early focus on culture, employee engagement, and customer service is vital.

We've covered the importance of creating a great place to work for employees, which is the first big step toward providing great service.

What often gets lost in the taproom model is that the service and customer experience provided at the bar are just as important as creating that tasty product. Without distribution, you are the manufacturer, the distributor, *and* the retailer all rolled into one. Consistent negative experiences from customers can impact a taproom-focused brewery in significant ways over time.

The Brewers Association, headed up by Tim Brady of Whetstone Station, provides a robust Customer Service Manual for member breweries. Brady gives fantastic talks about service at the Craft Brewers Conference each year and has plenty of great content when it comes to providing a terrific experience.

Here are some things we emphasize with our incredible staff at Perfect Plain Brewing Company.

1. **Attitude, attitude, attitude.**

   If you can't bring a great attitude to work, I have no room for you. It's everything in service. Every single person is coming into our taproom either to 1) have a great time or 2) take their mind off a bad day. Neither case allows any room for a bad attitude behind the bar or in the brewing area. Every employee has their bad days, but it's important to communicate to them that when those bad days come, they need to be open about them and discuss it with the manager. I would rather be short-staffed by one than to put a bad attitude behind our bar any day of the week.

   More important, you can't tolerate bad attitude with one staff member, then reprimand another. You or your manager needs to be vigilant about not permitting bad mojo at work.

2. **"Is this your first time here?"**

   This is one of my favorite front-of-house activators. If the person who walks into the taproom isn't a blatantly obvious regular, and even if you're kind of sure they've been in before, always ask, "Is this your first time here?" Either answer sets your taproom staff up for success. "No" means you can say, "Great, let me tell you about what's new on the menu today." "Yes" means "Great, let me walk you through our options and what we're about here at Perfect Plain."

3. **Someone will ask what you make that tastes like Bud Light. Embrace it.**

   Sure, it's low-hanging fruit to make fun of our less sophisticated customers. Here in the Deep South, we still have male customers refuse to drink a beer out of a Toscana glass because it has a stem and that's too "girly." But if you aren't looking at these inexperienced craft beer customer interactions as both gifts and opportunities to grow your business, you're letting ego get in the way.

   The reality is that – depending on location, of course – lighter styles will be near the top sellers in your taproom. We're seeing more and more trends to lighter styles both in craft and other disrupters of craft. When that customer asks what you have that tastes like Bud Light, that should be your key to put them into your light lager or Kölsch, while also coming back with a sample of that next step up on the ladder – perhaps a Pilsner with a little more bite. If executed correctly, you can curate this beginner to craft beer on their initial journey, which will forever tie that customer with loyalty to your establishment.

Sure, it's easier to make fun of that person, but it's more fun for revenue, tip money, and your brand to turn that beginner into *your* regular. If you don't, the brewery around the corner will treat that person right and keep their business forever.

4. Empower taproom staff to Do the Right Thing.

My favorite brewery job interview question is: "When was the last time you broke the rules because you thought it was the right thing to do?" I like to see how someone reacts and get a measure of their values.

At Perfect Plain our bartenders have a $25 tab per shift to use at their discretion. It's a regular's birthday? Someone didn't like their beer or bought a to-go bottle and it's flat? They've got dollars to comp at their own discretion, no questions asked. No approvals needed, just merely log the use into the POS system.

If we're going to say we want all employees to have an ownership mentality but they have to call a manager just to give away a $6 beer, are we really telling them we trust them? We tell our staff to trust their judgment and use that money to do the right thing for our guests and their experience.

The expectation is not that the employee will max out the $25 on every shift (and if so, we'd have a discussion). But not only do we want our customers to be happy as soon as possible, we also want to empower our staff to feel as if they are trusted with decisions.

What if I don't trust my staff to use it in the right way? That means you've got culture issues and it's time to look in the mirror and ask yourself if that employee you don't trust should be working here. Be sure and refer to the employee culture chapters in Part III for more help.

5. Pay for spilled beers (most of the time).

We all know that the gross margin on draught beer is quite high, and that empowers us to be able to be more forgiving and leverage that product and its perceived value to the customer for impact.

So, if a non-inebriated customer spills a full beer on the way back to their table, have your staff replace it free of charge. That beer that cost the brewery maybe 25 to 75 cents to manufacture will have reverberating positive financial impact from the story that customer will tell on social media, or even just their friends at a dinner party. When they say they spilled a beer, and without asking, the nice bartender at your brewery replaced it, that's way, way more valuable than those nickels you paid for it.

There is no metric anyone can show me that would dissuade me from considering this a stellar financial investment in the happiness of your customer and the power of your brand.

6. **Treat customer complaints as gifts.**

   While we've been fortunate to build strong ratings on every customer review site, when we do get a complaint one of the most common ones is that "it took 15 minutes to get a drink."

   Now the petty, defensive side of me wants to get that person's e-mail address, ask them the exact time they were in our taproom, spend two unproductive hours of my time to find them on the surveillance cameras during their visit, download said footage and send them, via certified mail, a thumb drive that shows in fact they waited not 15, but three minutes for a drink. Fifteen minutes is a very long time not to be served and here's proof, moron!

   Then my sanity finally kicks in.

   As the saying goes, would you rather be right or happy? As Quint said earlier, often we're blinded by wanting to be right. That's our ego talking. While I know that person who complained about 15 minutes is dead wrong, that's a gift – let's remind our staff to give some sense of duration to guests when things are busy: "Hey guys, welcome! I'll be with you in about three minutes. Thanks for coming in!"

   Let's listen, apologize and be kind.

6a. **Type your response to negative e-mails and internet reviews. Then pause.**

   After you've written your response, hit the pause button for at least 12 hours. We've all been blinded with rage about an unfair review. I've never said to myself, "*I should have sent that jerk response sooner!*" Give yourself a chance to regain your composure, and thank the person (genuinely) for the feedback. One of our favorite lines is: "Thank you for the opportunity to get better." It disarms the angry guest and shows restraint and professionalism to the lurkers who are reading the review.

7. **Be specific as possible about duration.**

   We all use clichés like "I'll be there in a second," or "I'll be right with you."

   That's not true. We won't be there in one second. We aren't literally right with them.

   Try to be specific about a clear expectation of time. A Denver brewery, Black Project, did this quite well when we were in town recently, explaining how their guest tap Pilsner was a slow pour that might take 2–3 minutes. When you prepare your guests for a small wait, they are more than likely happy to oblige. When you leave your customers hanging, that's when the anxiety raises, and negativity begins.

   We try to remember to say. "Hey, we're changing a keg; it will be about 3 minutes and I'll have your beer ready for you." Again, don't hesitate to be specific about duration.

8. **Involve brew-side staff in the customer experience.**

   This is a very common miss in the customer experience. People will want to talk to your brewing staff about what they are working on, what they are brewing next, techniques, and all sorts of things. I know, your brewing staff didn't sign up to interact with customers, right? Or they aren't the most social people, maybe?. Doesn't matter in my eyes. In the taproom experience, that's a secondary part of the job. Perhaps the brewers don't need to be as excellent as your bar staff on the friendliness scale, but you wouldn't prevent the bar staff from learning about the beer if they said, "Well, we aren't brewers." I don't see why brew-side staff shouldn't be involved in at least part of the front-of-house training.

We're equal opportunity cross trainers as well. All bar staff is required to go through a brew day within their first 90 days and one more time during the year. There are all sorts of ways to make that transaction fun, such as bartender beer tasting contests and much more.

Chapter 21

How to Program Your Taproom to Build Revenue

Bryant Liggett, Perfect Plain Events and Marketing Manager, and D.C. Reeves

IF AT NO other time, we're reminded just how valuable programming is each and every February when zombies and hobbits and ghouls take over our taproom. We transform the taproom for Pensacon, a week-long regionalized version of the famous Comic-Con. That transformation, done with such spirit by our marketing and events manager and resident uber-nerd at Perfect Plain, Events and Marketing Manager Bryant "BB" Liggett, brings an added layer of intrigue, fun, and revenue into our building. We also brew a special beer, feature locally crafted commemorative beer steins, and release bottles as collector's items specific to our theme that given year.

Does it take time to decorate? Of course. Does it take time to plan and do it right? Of course. But there are so many wins that come with programming.

Programming is the regular scheduling of events, both large and small, done internally by a brewery to attract customers to your taproom. The most obvious examples are live music, trivia nights, and beer specials. That's programming at its most basic level.

What does programming do? It introduces our company and taproom to new people. We show that we support our community and its big happenings – that we're hip to what's going on in our market – and it builds our reputation and our brand.

Programming comes both big (Pensacon) and small (trivia night, pint night, etc.). Both are valuable for building a customer base, bringing in new customers, and giving your community more reasons to come in. Without programming, it's like a brewery sits on its hands and expects busy people with busy lives to come to them instead of the competition. That's not a safe assumption.

Who says we aren't all into programming? PPBC bartender Chrissy Helvenston takes a devilishly good beer order during the Lord of the Rings Pensacon Event in 2019.

But we challenge you to think outside the box when programming your taproom. Nothing wrong with live music – we use it all the time – but I wouldn't end my programming efforts there. With so much available at our fingertips yelling for our attention, consumers nowadays expect more, and different, and inspired programming to garner attention.

The DO's of Programming

1. **Know your brand.** First and foremost, know your brand. Know your guests. Make sure your event ideas fit the brand and scope of your space and your supporters. Define success and determine your event expectations. Ask yourself, "What's our 'why' behind this?" "Who's our target audience?" "What are we trying to accomplish?" "Will this event speak to our guests and align with our values?" Determining these elements is the foundation to every successful event.

2. **Construct unique and notable experiences.** Research, research, research. Be mindful of the styles of events that are working in your neighborhood and your city, and then try something new.

What hasn't been done yet? Be unusual. Use your imagination. Push boundaries. Don't be afraid to try new things. Creativity and attention to detail are primary elements in every event (with a little absurdity thrown in there, too).

3. **Make your events as memorable as your beer ... and not *just* about beer.** To be a true communal hub means that not every event is tied to beer (beer specials, beer releases, etc.). We love collaborating with our community and like-minded organizations. Pensacon, Pensacola's week-long, regional-sized version of Comic-Con, is one of our favorite local collaborations. The partnership aligns with our brand, speaks to our guests, and gives us a chance to push the boundaries of nerdism. Each year we choose a pop culture theme, co-brand a bottle release, and decorate our taproom in this theme for an entire week. This particular event is not just about the beer, but about a bigger picture; it's about community spirit, collaboration, and overall experience. And it reflects in our taproom sales.

4. **Keep 'em coming back for more.** What drives repeat customers? One-off events are awesome, but establishing reoccurring weekly, monthly, and yearly programming is a key element to taproom success. Whether it's a weekly pint night, live music, or trivia night, driving these events to the forefront of guest's minds is the most important part in programming, particularly when they occur on slower days of the week. Utilize social media by creating a recurring Facebook Event. Continuously post updates in the discussion feed. This minimizes the work of having to create a new event each week and keeps your social media footprint active.

    Other ways to spread the word about events: Posters, rack cards in your check presenters, and Instagram stories are easy ways to keep your programming seen, and guests coming back for more. Do you have a weekly crowler special? Educate your staff to communicate that special to the guest who stops by after work to take home a crowler: "Hey, I know you like to enjoy your beer at home, so don't forget that every Tuesday we do discounted crowlers. You should stop by then!" The guest appreciates that you remember his or her tendencies and in two sentences you've created a new Tuesday regular.

5. **Communicate extensively with your employees and guests.** We've discussed this before in relations to other facets, but it's no different

in programming. Communication – bordering on overcommunication– is important to generate excitement about your events with both guests *and* staff. If your staff is excited, they'll get your guests excited. Communicate with your staff regarding every event. Make sure they know the event's *why*. Create a BEO (banquet event order) containing detailed information regarding each event. Make sure they are readily accessible in the taproom so staff can answer any question they may not have an answer to. Educate your staff.

BEO	
Prepared By:	**BB**
Date Booked:	12.2.18
EVENT INFORMATION	
Event Name:	Surprise Birthday Party
Event Date:	12.22.18
Start Time:	6:30
End Time:	11PM
Event Type:	Surprise Party
Number of Guests:	20
Guarantee/Minimum Spend/Rental Fee:	N/A
Location:	Rachel Table + High Top
CLIENT INFORMATION	
Main Contact:	Jesse Breedlove
Email:	N/A
Phone Number:	(850) 555-5555
EVENT DETAILS	

Event Notes:

- Owners of Rusted Arrow Mercantile
- Surprise party for his wife, Sam
- Reserve the Rachel Table + a 6 top - put into the shape of a "T"
- Reserve a high-top table next to the Christmas tree (for cupcakes)
- He will bring by small decorations (balloons, sign, etc).
- He is paying for Jordan that night

Bar Details:

- Open Bar, no limitations
- Jesse will start a tab with a card when he gets here
- His guests will let you know they're on the Breedlove tab

Menu Details:

- He's having pizzas delivered at 7:45

6. **Scale event size and frequency.** Programming oversaturation can happen! It's important to be realistic about what your staff and taproom can handle. It's more important to have fewer, more tailored events than high-frequency thrown-together events. Is April a slower month for you? Take a look at your year-over-year monthly sales to see which have been historically busier or slower. A slower time may be better for a large, detailed event that you can spend more time crafting into something special that will garner interest and excitement in the community. Scale your event size and frequency to match the amount of time and effort you can put into it. Labor hours are an expense as well, so when you start tabulating the time and cost to execute, be sure you're factoring in the potential return on investment – either sales, brand awareness, cool factor, or a combination of all three. At PPBC we've had events that took 10 percent of the time of others that were bigger wins than the larger-scale events. So bigger is not always better when you're programming quality events.

The DON'T's of Programming

1. **Deep discount nights.** Think back to your early 20s, long, long ago. There's a bar you remember that had 50-cent or $1 beers on a certain night of the week. You were there a *lot* on that one night (or was that just us?)

   Now ask yourself – how often did you go to that bar on any of the other nights and pay $4 or $5 for a beer? Rarely. Why? Because the bars you love frequenting on busier nights of the week, with the livelier crowds and greater ambiance, didn't *need* to discount their beer to 50 cents to get crowds.

Events That Have Worked for Us at Perfect Plain

Pensacon. This week-long comic convention celebration is not only one of our most successful events, but also one of the most fun. It's one of our largest and attracts the highest volume of guests, and thus requires the greatest amount of planning, marketing, budgeting, and time. Each year we collaborate with Pensacon and choose a theme (2018, The Walking Dead; 2019, Lord of the Rings), release a themed barrel-aged bottle, and decorate the taproom with themed decor, beer, cocktails, and costumes. Some of the mini-events include the Official Pensacon Kick-Off Party, Annual Bottle Release, Themed Trivia Night, Drink and Draw with professional comic book artists, and more. Pensacon itself brings big dollars to our downtown economy. With 60,000 annual attendees, it boosts tourism, increases the vibrancy of our little city, and brings together like-minded individuals in our area. Our partnership with Pensacon is so, so valuable to us and our guests. It's the perfect avenue to introduce our product to wide genre of guests from near and far.

Drag Show and Glitter Beer Release. I can't stress this enough: *think outside the box!* This event is one of our favorites. It's one of the easiest, most fun, and highest guest volume events we throw. We did a baby brite of one-night-only glitter beer, then I coordinated with our local drag queens, hired a DJ, and planned a drag show and release party. We had huge response on Facebook the instant it was announced. Local thematic vendors set up shop in the taproom, our cocktail program is glitter-themed for the evening, and our guests and staff have an incredible time. This is also a great way to participate in a local human rights charity drive.

Halloween Pet Costume Contest. We love that our taproom is pet friendly! And because of this, we're always trying to

(continued)

(continued)

find ways to incorporate dogs into our programming. Every Halloween we invite a panel of guest judges from local animal shelters, set up a red carpet and photo booth, and pups and their owners walk the runway for a chance to win prizes for pups (spent grain treats, PPBC dog merch) and their humans (beer)!

Star Wars Day. *May the 4th Be with You.* As you can probably tell, we love to nerd out! Our yearly *Star Wars* beer release, Binary Sunset IIPA, is the main focal point for this day. We decorate our taproom, craft a themed cocktail menu, and host a *Star Wars* trivia night and costume contest. It's an awesome, low-key but high-guest-volume day that everyone loves.

Source: BB Liggett, Events and Marketing Manager, PPBC.

So often in the bar and restaurant industry, when companies get desperate for revenue, they fall into the trap of deep discounts. It may work on that one night, but the hidden consequence is that – especially with a brewery making its own product – you have now devalued your product the rest of the nights.

Consumers will silently be asking themselves: *Why should I pay $6 for this beer when it's $1.25 on another night?* Once a product is devalued, it is very difficult to recover its stature.

If you want more revenue, instead of cutting prices, add programming, and do "take home a pint glass" nights that create value instead of reducing price.

We're not recommending that you never offer discounts. We do it during hurricane parties (when a hurricane is making landfall close to us) and on other one-off special occasions. Just don't make a habit of discounts of a half off or more. What you make now will cost more than you think later.

2. **Don't get desperate for events – in or outside your taproom.** This falls under the same category as knowing your brand. If Perfect Plain was hosting a weekly book club or a cigar club that brought 10 people in, but they spent the entire time shushing or smoking out our taproom guests, what are we gaining? Just like you shouldn't get desperate for discounts, never get desperate enough to take just any event.

    Same goes for offsite beer festivals. There are widely varying opinions in our industry on this, but the truth is that preparing for a beer festival is a lot of work. Sometimes the beer you pour is not purchased but offered for free.

    The appetite for offsite festivals will change rapidly with the growth of your company. In the pre-open days it makes sense to test product and meet as many people as possible. As the brewery grows, time gets more valuable and most breweries start to become much pickier about where they go. Perfect Plain is open to pouring at festivals, but with the exception of local festivals put on by close friends of the brewery, we rarely pour at local or regional events when the beer isn't purchased at least at some price. It's not about the money, but 1) we are a taproom only so it's really only a branding gain for us in whatever amount, and 2) the brewery has to give so much time, equipment usage, and other sacrifices to be offsite for an entire day (if not more) that we don't see it as a mutual win if the festival organizers aren't willing to offset any of that cost for us.

    In the case of Great American Beer Fest or other nationally or internationally prestigious festivals, we make the cost-benefit analysis of exposure and experience for our staff and brand to be there versus the cost to pull it off. When it makes sense, we go for it.

    We aren't offering exact rules, because these all depend on your brewery's age, business model, and needs at the time. The important thing is to do that analysis and see if a festival asking for your participation is right for you.

Taproom Talk with Nic Pelaez, Director of Hospitality, Modern Times Beer Co., San Diego, California

1. What are your philosophical approach and key priorities to managing your taproom?

Our focus is on hiring – and retaining – amazing employee-owners who offer service to match our fantastic beers, food, and coffee. We feel that if we hire and train the right people, they will take care of our guests and create fans for life.

2. Your company has proven to be outside-the-box thinkers. How do you extrapolate that image to your brand in the taproom?

Instead of just focusing on the beer, we also place a huge emphasis on art, atmosphere, food, coffee, and service, which are often overlooked in the beer industry. By making those as much of a priority as the quality of beer, we differentiate ourselves from other breweries, restaurants, and bars while fostering a community that genuinely enjoys the space and comes back often.

3. If you could give advice to anyone running a taproom in America, what would it be?

Make hiring, training, retention, and service as much of a priority as brewing. Each employee is an ambassador of your brand and has a direct impact on your guests' experience. Employee satisfaction is directly correlated to guest satisfaction, so take care of your employees and make the success of the company relevant to their own personal success and career development.

4. How do you handle the balance between positioning the central product well – beer – and doing events or programming in the taproom that aren't built around beer?

Generally, we focus on planning events and programming that we'd be psyched about if we were outside the company, and then we work backward. If there is a tie-in with beer, food, or coffee – great. If not, we make sure it ties into tenets of our company philosophy, like social responsibility or inclusiveness.

5. How do you approach social media as far as bringing in taproom sales? How often do you post (or do you even have a policy on this), what do you try and post about, what's your vibe?

We typically post about new beers as they arrive, especially in the case of our more limited offerings. If it's something we're releasing in a canned or bottled format, we'll post a teaser with the artwork, since that's also something we get really excited about. We've been fortunate to have a ton of organic interest in our new and limited beers, so more often than not we're posting to let people know that they should get some while they can, or to get their thoughts on beers we're considering for wider release, rather than primarily as a sales push. As to what we post informationally, our basic philosophy is to offer the info that we – as beer nerds – would want to know before buying a beer. Process, ingredients, adjuncts, new or interesting processes, and, of course, tasting notes. As you can probably tell from this answer, we're not afraid to be a bit text-heavy.

6. What are your top pieces of advice or tips for creating a healthy work environment for your staff in a taproom?

Make your employees as much of a focus as the product or the guest. Make the success of the company tie into their own personal success, through something like employee-ownership or through their own career growth. Be transparent with them and share how they can directly impact the growth of the company. Be purposeful about asking for feedback from them on how you as a management team or as a company can improve.

7. How do you describe what makes a great employee?

We look for people with goals and values that align with ours. We want employee-owners who want to grow with the company, who would benefit from being a part of a fast-growing company, and who want to contribute to making our company fantastic.

Chapter 22

Keys to Improving Day-to-Day Taproom Operations

While I can speak to our experience, understand that these are guiding ideas and tools and can still be effective when modified. If you have a much smaller or much larger staff, it is understandable that the programming of meetings and the like may be less frequent. Still, try to instill some of these principles in your new or fledgling brewery operation.

Weekly "family" meetings. Set a single, one-hour, non-negotiable, regular meeting each week with your leaders. I'm amazed how few breweries actually set time aside time to meet; when we do collaboration brews on Mondays and they see what our meeting is like they usually say "we should start doing this!". In my view this is an absolute must. If you have a brewery and are not doing this, start doing this immediately.

Note that just talking with everyone at the brewery intermittently doesn't count as a "meeting." We're talking about dedicated time with a clear outcome. With no standard meeting time and each department in a silo, you will miss so many things: dropped balls on coordination, and – just as painful – missed opportunities to collaborate on ideas. If we are holding a big event in town and we want to have a beer to go with it, if our marketing/events person isn't talking with the brew side staff, we'll miss our chance to maximize the greatness of the event.

At Perfect Plain we meet every Monday at noon and include all people who supervise any staff. We go around to each bucket – Director of Brewing Operations, Head Brewer, Taproom Operations Manager, Marketing and Events Manager, Owner. We all give

156

updates, then table longer discussion topics until the end. We settle on our social media schedule for the week during these meetings.

We typically save disciplinary issues for the direct staff involved but announce any staff discipline or changes when ready at this meeting first before notifying all staff.

We also have an open-door policy for other staff who would like to sit in on a meeting at any time. as long as they give us notice in advance.

Monthly company-wide meetings. It's easy to get in the habit of not doing this, but one of the most common reasons someone leaves a company is that they feel disengaged or that they aren't being communicated with about the direction of the company.

We practice transparency as much as possible by letting all staff know about the goings on. I give updates on anything organizational, even if it has nothing to do with them. Does buying a new foeder impact the bartender's daily routine? No, but if the goal is for employees to be empowered and feel like owners, they should know what is going on. We ask all departments to give updates to all staff during these meetings. In addition, this is when we do additional training, and in many cases, we follow it up with lunch or something fun they can look forward to. Employees might complain about an early morning, but I consider this part of everyone's obligation to our company as an employee. It's not asking too much for all of the organization to follow our routine.

Quarterly outings for staff (that have nothing to do with work). Plan something that's fun *and* has no work component about it. Following the holiday season, we had a meeting in the morning at the brewery, then I arranged for every employee and their significant other to have a hotel room at Pensacola Beach for the night. BB planned beach Olympic games for staff, we bought everyone dinner, and went out together. It's an expense, of course, but I look at it purely as an investment in your people. Don't forget just how expensive it is to lose good people, both in time and in finances.

Create a Daily Report for the Closing Leader to Fill Out

Dovetailed into the importance of financial transparency with staff, a daily report that goes to all staff is extremely valuable. This is where the closing manager or bartender sends a document that shows the day's sales and other updates that are important to staff. Not only does it keep your employees in tune with your company's performance, but it also helps leadership react to any issues. We've been able to hop on concerns like broken trash cans, small equipment replacements, and other potential problem areas much faster because our bartenders are talking to us through this report each and every night.

Here is an example of what we call our "Rachel Report," named after Rachel Jackson, the wife of U.S. President Andrew Jackson. Rachel spent time in Pensacola and dubbed it the "Perfect Plain," in a letter from July 23, 1821, inspiring our name.

Rachel Report Template

GENERAL INFORMATION
Report Date:

Reporting Manager:

Holiday/Special Events:

Weather:

Entertainment:

SALES AND COUNTS
Total Sales:

Total Transactions:

Taproom Sales:

Gift Certificate Sales:

Merchandise Sales:

All Other Sales:

STAFFING
Number of Bartenders:

Trainee(s) / Name / Position / Training Day:

Was the level of staffing appropriate for the day?:

General Staffing Comments:
REPORTING INFORMATION

General Notes:

Any PPX in today? If so, who?:

Event Notes:

Food Truck/Food Service:

Guest Comments:

Who did a good job today? Who do we need to recognize? What did they do?:

Were there any incidents that happened today?

Product Quality Feedback:

Lost and Found:

Items 86'd

Did any kegs kick? If so, which ones?:

Repairs and Maintenance

To Do–Misc Notes for BB or Brewers:

Is the office / keg room tidy?

Daily/Weekly Sidework Completed?

perfectplain
Perfect Plain Brewing Co.   ...

View Insights   Promote

Liked by **thomas3times** and **203 others**

perfectplain Given our current obsession of wood aging and barrel fermentation, we found it strikingly fitting that we should be hosting the Archaeo Cafe event this evening to talk about barrels that have been uncovered by archaeologists in downtown Pensacola! This event is open to the public and begins at 6:00p. See you there!

View 1 comment

AUGUST 29, 2018

Condition Leadership to Look at Sales Trends

The books are not just for accountants. Something as basic as keeping an eye on the previous year's or month's sales trends can be helpful as you grow. Should a brewery open early on holidays like Memorial Day or Veterans Day? Should they stay open later on the night before since it's a holiday? With a simple check of your point-of-sale system, leaders can see how sales fared the previous year and react. Combine that knowledge with a daily report (if executed and filled out correctly by bar staff) and you have plenty of decision-making power at your fingertips.

We have come across situations where we have been able to anticipate different hours, including times when we realized it would not be worth opening early.

Leadership should always have a strong understanding of your average per-day sales. We do about 50–55 percent of our sales on weekends and about 75–80 percent of our sales Thursday–Sunday. That should be top of mind with all management staff. Why? That should factor into all sorts of revenue-based decisions.

1. When should you book private events, and what should you charge based on the day requested? (Until the expansion was complete, we refused to rent our space on weekends because it was cost prohibitive for what we would need to charge to make it be a feasible business decision for us.)
2. When should you be booking events because sales are slower? A common practice in taprooms is to close on Mondays and schedule only private events on those days. Get a feel for what your Mondays are like and adjust accordingly. We have chosen to be open seven days per week, and we try to guide all private event rentals into the first four days of the week.
3. When should you *not* book events because sales are strong?

Keep an eye on the fluctuation in sales of merchandise and wine/liquor as well. If those numbers sag, it's nice to know so you can order fresh merchandise, offer some specials, and pivot your social media strategy accordingly to bring awareness. Again, you can't fix what you aren't measuring.

Who's Going to Own This?

How many meetings have you been in where you walk out after an hour of talking about projects and you don't know who's in charge? As mentioned earlier, eliminate ambiguity and designate who is going to own everything. I can't count how many times I've heard Quint say, "80 percent of failure is ambiguity."

Who's owning social media this week? Who's owning that post on Memorial Day?

Who's owning the review of the brew-side SOPs?

Who's going to let the staff know about our new drink specials?

Don't leave a meeting without someone being the owner of each action item.

Involve Your Staff in Planning and Ideas Other Than Work

Our bartender Sarah has created a side business doing body glitter for events around the area. Our bartender Chrissy owns her own small business doing flowers for events and weddings. Our bartender Derek likes learning about the cocktail side of things and puts in hours juicing and related activities to learn. Our bartender Billy is thinking about getting into the insurance adjustment business.

Know what your employees' *what* is and help feed their passions outside of work. As mentioned before, we provided that $250 stipend to them to spend on other skill building that they love.

Require All Leaders to Highlight Someone in the Company Doing Something Great Once Per Month.

Owners can't have their finger on the pulse of their company every moment of every day. It's easy to miss that employee who put in two 14-hour days in a week because they care about the company. Rely on your leaders to report about someone who has done a standout job and why. That way, the owner can send a personal thank you note to that staff member (to their home, and not just a text message!) and also let that staffer know which leader pointed them out.

Now the employee feels good about the owner, the company, and their direct supervisor.

Don't Ever, Ever Be Cash Only

Yes, credit card fees suck. They do. Toilet paper isn't a fun purchase either, but you aren't thinking about cutting that out of your budget, are you? Thinking about cutting hops out of your budget? We do between 85 and 90 percent of our business through credit cards at Perfect Plain.

It's called the cost of doing business. And believe it or not, there are still breweries not taking credit cards.

Think about asking your customers to pay a $2 to $4 fee on an ATM in your building (of which the brewery gets merely a fraction). Then, they take out their money, already perturbed by this transaction, and likely on principal whatever they take out is their best-case scenario budget for your taproom. (I'm not sure there's a beer in the U.S. I would pay two ATM transaction fees for.) Your average ticket will most certainly suffer, and that doesn't even factor in the sales you are losing because people never come in your door once aware of this annoyance.

Pay the credit card fees. It's worth it. Be sure to shop around – we've already changed companies once by shopping for a better rate that saved us thousands. But just pay it.

Nowadays it is getting more and more popular for companies to pass on their transaction fee to the customer. I'm still not a believer in trading money for the potential feeling you can give customers – and if you're that desperate for the additional 2 to 3 percent, I've got a better idea: up your prices by 2.5%. Studies show that any fractional price increase, handled smartly, won't even be noticed by customers.

Chapter 23

The Value of Finding and Preserving Mentorship

MENTORSHIP IS VALUABLE in so many ways when someone is starting or growing their business.

It's learning from someone who has been successful, learning from someone who has made mistakes, and learning from someone who can identify barriers and see around corners because of all that experience.

It's safe to assume already that it's valuable to you – it's the same reason you are motivated to read this book. We all have that thirst to know we're on the right path or doing the right thing.

We're additionally blessed to be in an industry where collaboration is the norm. "Competing" breweries are much more likely to help with lending a tool or part or trading those hops on a whim. I don't think most restaurants would say the same thing. I put this chapter in customer experience, because so much of mentorship in our industry isn't just how we treat customers, but the kind of experience we provide to our fellow independent craft breweries. We're all in this together, and sometimes that gets lost.

The takeaway for this chapter is that if you're willing to put in some time, it is much easier to get a mentor than you may think. I'll share some tips on how to cultivate that relationship later.

My story and mentorship in business really starts with three people: my father, Jim Reeves; my boss, Quint Studer; and Bert Thornton.

My father was a real estate attorney in Pensacola who was involved in many facets of different businesses, from ownership to partnership to board of director positions. My parents divorced when I was young, so during my time with Dad it was normal for me to sit in the back of bank board meetings, law firm staff meetings, and Tuesday morning Rotary Club breakfasts before school. Those meetings would be catalysts for my wondering mind, and I learned a lot about business from my father by watching him and asking a lot of questions.

Later in life, outside of family, I hit the mentor lottery.

Quint taught me everything I know about the value of employee and company culture, about how to lead a business, and about how to do the right thing, even when it is difficult.

It was Quint's job offer in 2015 that brought me back to Pensacola, and the constant evolution of my role with him over these few years has allowed me to do impactful work and learn from one of the best. His influence and proven track record of pioneering customer service in our nation's healthcare industry has been modified and retrofitted for our little company and has worked wonders for us. Our turnover is way below industry averages and our employee happiness – which we track annually – is in the 95th percentile of companies of our size - brewery or not - nationwide.

Not only did I earn some sort of informal, undocumented MBA merely by working for Quint and watching him do what he does best with some of the nation's most prominent businesses, but I dread even to think that I would have opened Perfect Plain without knowing what I know now. It's this point alone that makes me passionate about writing this book. I want to pass a lot of this knowledge that has been so helpful to me into the hands of every brewery so they can be a better organization, especially since so few breweries actually take the time to focus on the development of their company and their people. To steal a Quint-ism, "Often the owner spends so much time working *in* the business that they forget to work *on* the business."

I certainly would not have been able to write this book about best practices and address issues like company culture, hiring, customer service, and day-to-day operations in the same way without him.

I consider myself fortunate to have those connections in my life that taught me so much.

Yes, I can hear your brain now: "You're lucky. I don't have people like that in my life to help me!"

First off, you're right, I am lucky. But secondly, let me tell you about my third mentor, Bert, whom I didn't know, had no connection to, and had never met. I just e-mailed and asked him if I could buy him lunch one day.

Bert Thornton, the Vice President Emeritus of Waffle House Inc., spent decades of his decorated business career in Atlanta, but semi-retired down to the Pensacola area a few years ago. He's the namesake of "Bert's Chili," inside every Waffle House. As you saw, he wrote the foreword for this book.

When I heard he had moved into the area following his semi-retirement after more than four decades, I just took a shot and reached out to him in 2016. After a little while, he wrote back and agreed to meet with me for lunch.

Shockingly, we met at a Waffle House. I told him most of my previous Waffle House experience came after 10 p.m.

Keep in mind, Bert owed me nothing. He didn't know who I was, or really what I did, or what entrepreneurial project I had in mind. He was generous with his time, and a great listener.

We had maybe five or six lunches during my planning stages of Perfect Plain. We talked about everything. He asked questions I didn't have answers to, but quickly made a point to find them.

Near the end, I asked him the big favor of reading my 41-page business plan to see what concerns he had. He called me about a week later after reading every single word – no exaggeration, I think he may have read it more intently than I did.

He gave me grammatical edits on page 26. He questioned my math and logic on building some numbers. It was invaluable and something I'll never forget.

And it's safe to say I walked into those meetings with lenders with high confidence (and a couple extra pounds thanks to all those hash browns) that my plan and projections were sound, thanks to Bert.

We still talk every month or so, and he's great about bringing friends in to get crowlers to go. I'm proud to call him a mentor and friend.

Keys to Being a Good Mentee

- **The onus is on you to initiate.** The best mentors out there, not coincidentally, have a *lot* going on. Don't expect a brilliant business or brewery mind to come knock on your door and ask to help. Be bold. Reach out to people in your community. Again, you'll be shocked how many people would not only be willing to help but would be flattered you asked.

- **It doesn't have to be a "beer" person.** Don't think it has to be someone who is already a brewery owner. And in some cases, it's better that it's not. For better or worse, for the more insider industry knowledge a beer person has, at the end of the day you may be competing with them.

- **Mind the relationship.** As Bert has written in his book, *Finding an Old Gorilla* – a great and easy read that addresses mentorship in depth – mentorship is a two-way street. If you treat it as sponging information with no plan to mind the relationship, it will falter. Send thank you notes. Send texts or e-mails specifically when you aren't asking for something.

- **Be prepared.** Treat these meetings almost like a job interview. Dress appropriately. Know your stuff. One better – I would ask your mentor ahead of time what they would be interested in seeing (a pro-forma, a business plan, etc.). If you're having lunch with your mentor one day and they ask about some data you don't have, be prepared to follow up and share that the next time you meet. Why? It shows that you value their feedback and don't just blow it off the second you leave your meeting. That shows your mentor that you have drive and that you're doing something with the time they are investing in you.

- **Pay it forward.** It is practically guaranteed that someone else opening a brewery will reach out to you for help. That's not to say you're obligated to share your secret sauce, but how many times have you read about a brewery shutting down because the old one helped the new one? Do the right thing and certainly your kindness and willingness to grow quality craft beer culture will follow.

Chapter 24

Best Practices Q&A: Burial Beer Co. Co-Founder Doug Reiser

BACK IN 2013, the idea of opening Burial Beer Co. was that it would just be a side hustle for Doug Reiser, his wife, Jess, and their friend Tim Gormley. Six years later, Burial has established itself as one of the strongest independent craft beer brands in Asheville, North Carolina. The Reisers and Gormley started as a one-barrel system, quickly ditched that to keep up with demand, and have grown to become one of the leading names in craft in the United States. One of their biggest assets was the litany of vast experience in their ownership team. Doug, a former attorney, spoke with me about their journey through growing Burial in the taproom, the state of the industry, and key things to watch out for as you get your business off the ground.

D.C. Reeves: Take us through the process of getting Burial open. What did you guys feel like you nailed? What did you struggle with? What do you remember most?

Doug Reiser: This is a really good time to talk about this. We've been doing a lot of reflection on our vision and trying to divorce ourselves from tradition. I think a lot of businesses get stuck in something they did early on, and you just get attached to it. A lot of breweries, I think, really live and die by either being willing or unwilling to change and adapt and divorce themselves from things that have become stagnant or stale. A lot of breweries are just committed to the things they started with, and they think that there's some type of equity in those things. They want to see them through. In today's world, with thousands and thousands of breweries, whatever's new and shiny seems to always be what works. For us, with Burial, when we opened as the one-barrel (brewhouse), we didn't care what we made. Not a lot of thought went into it on the consumer side. Everything was pure, unadulterated creativity, whatever the hell we wanted to make for ourselves. When you're making a barrel of beer at a time, it's going to get sold, it doesn't matter. People are just excited. We had such little beer that people were going to be excited about anything that we made. We also didn't really have any recognizable persona or a public reputation. Any consumer who walked in the door was just excited to be there, drinking anything.

Early on, the reason we opened Burial was really as a hobby project. My wife, Tim, and I all had different careers. Tim was a logistics guy for a while. I was an attorney. I also owned a software company at the same time. That was really my paycheck. We figured we would just do it on the weekend, and it was just going to be a totally fun, experimental showcase thing. As long as it made enough money to pay for itself, then we were happy. That's why we did the one barrel in a crappy little space in the South Slope of Asheville, and at the time South Slope didn't even exist. It was just kind of a place for prostitutes and druggies.

Sometimes great things come from that organic place. I think consumers can smell intention, trying to be intentionally cool. We were just haphazardly cool, because we didn't have any money. We were totally broke, and we just took what we had and put that out there. We were crappy because that's all we could afford. We just left the place the way it was. We made super rustic beer because we had a very, very inexpensive brewhouse. We had ambient fermenters. We focused a lot on making beers that could taste good, ambiently fermented. Thus, we made a lot of farmhouse beer and Belgian beer. We made some higher-gravity beers. We made IPA, of course. We actually had a little chamber so that we could make lager. We opened with two lagers, and I think after we opened, we never had another lager for almost nine months because we just could never do that and keep our doors open on a one-barrel system. I remember we had three one-barrel tanks and a two-barrel tank. That two-barrel tank was our IPA tank.

It was at a time where I felt like a full portfolio was a Saison, a Belgian, a stout or two, maybe another Saison, an IPA, and a lager. I think a lot of breweries open that way: "This is what's in my head as stuff that I think is cool." It's less like what you think people want to buy, but more what you think is cool. What might cut your ego.

DC: You mention ego, and it's something I discuss regularly in the book – the balance between the holistic, creative process that attracts people into beer and brewing, and the notion of creating a sustainable business. For example, the balance of not wanting to undermine the craft and make 12 light beers that won't fill your passion for creativity, but not sinking your ship with 12 styles no one in your market wants – especially at the taproom level. Finding that balance. How did you guys do that?

DR: A lot of startup brewers have that problem. It's kind of a curse, really. We all have egos as homebrewers, or a brewer in a brewery who's actually doing what's right and selling things that consumers want. I think brewers who work in those environments sometimes, commercially, get stagnant on what they're putting out all the time, and they want something different from that, different from the norm. Homebrewers as well.

A lot of brewers, I think, open with that idea, that they're just going to make something different to be different. We definitely were that, but it didn't hurt us, because we were making beer for the few. When you're that small, you're making beer for the few. Even when we decided to expand into the pub and put a 10-barrel in there, and buy the property, and create some outdoor space that we could host more people . . . Asheville, at the same time, kind of took off. South Slope grew and became a tourism center.

We had so many people coming in, tourists, and we were still making 10 barrels of beer at a time. We still felt like we could make whatever the hell we wanted, but we quickly realized that our IPAs were disappearing really fast, and that people actually did want to drink lager. We made more of those beers, but by and large, as the pub, we were very much still committed to being esoteric as much as possible. I think it had value.

A lot of people, to this day, really love the fact that we were weird, off the cuff, trying weird ingredients, making beers that were sometimes super polarizing, that were certainly just small sample sippers, not "pint after pint" beers. In that time frame, that worked for us, and we found a lot of success with it.

DC: Selfishly, I look at Burial as a benchmark for my own brewery because of that "yin-yang" ownership similarity that we both have, albeit at a much younger age in our life cycle of our brewery than you guys are today. Having decision makers and owners at the table who understand and respect the quality of beer and bring business acumen to the table, too. An ownership structure that has the capacity to think with our hearts as well as our heads.

I think, in a lot of industries – not just craft beer, but also restaurants, bakeries – the technician opens the brewery, or the baker opens the bakery a lot of the time. That, perhaps, is sometimes a missing piece when you see breweries that are not successful or do something because they think that's what they should do. Or ego. You mentioned a lot of that.

How are you guys able to navigate that, and do you think that that kind of partnership of having somebody who already had owned a business, who had worked in a different field and wants to open a brewery – was that a valuable thing for you guys?

DR: There's a lot there. Just to start it, I think no business is successful without a vision. You have to have visionaries. We are fortunate and also cursed to have two visionaries. I think you're right. The baker who opens the bakery, at some point, as they garner success and attention, a lot of different pressures get put on them. "Do I just commit to what I know, and just keep doing that, even knowing that I'm limiting myself?" "Do I take advantage of opportunity?" But if you take advantage of opportunity, you can't grow with wild, fleeting passion. It's got to be done with business sense and reality, and fiscal responsibility.

Yeah, Tim and I shared visionary roles at Burial, and it has worked for a very long time in a very good way. I think that, as we have gotten to the scale that we're at now is, for the first time we're really having to sit down and be like, "All right. What are we doing? Are we just going to keep putting things out that are totally a product of our personal passions and desires, or are we putting out things that our customers demand?" That has been a negotiation. That has been something where you have to sit down.

Tim and I are very yin and yang. We have very many comparable traits that are awesome, and that's why we've been such great partners. For instance, the number one priority for both of us is beer quality. If it's not absolutely great, it doesn't exist on a Burial brand. Have we compromised that before? Hell yeah. We've definitely made things that were maybe good for their purpose, but not good for our customer base, if that makes sense. Maybe you make things that you personally absolutely adore, but your customer base isn't going to adore them. We're at a point now where people see a Burial name, they expect the best. That's not me being cocky or anything, that's just the reality.

We are a brewery with the attention of the national beer scene, of course, but even as we've started doing things internationally in Europe and beyond, all that does is make the stakes higher, in that people expect every single beer that you make to end up on Untappd as a four-point-something. You fall short of that, and you really feel the hurt. You lose customers right away. You get one shot sometimes with these guys when the expectations are that high.

With us putting beer out there into the marketplace, at some point, there was a movement, where everybody who drank our beer was drinking it at our place. We controlled the message. We controlled the narrative of what the beer was, the purpose behind it. We controlled the quality of it. If you didn't like the first one, you could try 12 other ones, to a model where we have beer out there everywhere. We really don't even know. I'm in New York City right now, and I'm about to go visit 30 different places where our beer is on tap. They're buying one keg every couple months. It's selling in New York. Everything's a 10-ounce pour, so there's 120 people who are going to try that beer. That's their one Burial experience, potentially. You have to think about that.

Sometimes at that scale and that risk level, you can't necessarily afford to just throw caution to the wind and wax your ego and put out a weird one-sided beer that's super polarizing. The description lines on tap lists at restaurants are like, "Name of beer" and "style." They don't have your whole story. They don't talk about that time you visited Mont Blanc and you tried wormwood off of the bush, and you decided to put it in.

You have to be cognizant of that, and I think we are. We're very careful now about what we send out into the marketplace, ensuring that they are beers that we are very proud of, that are ubiquitous enough to please the bulk of our audience.

People expect us to make really good IPA, and we make really crushable lager. We make some cool mixed-culture saison, and some unique dark beers. I think that that's what we know we murder, and we want to continue to get those beers out. We know can use the taproom as a place for experimentation, because we control the narrative there, and that it's a marginal impact on the consumer if it is so polarizing.

In general, what I would say is, yes, of the two visionaries at Burial, I am much more business minded. That is good for us, and it is also very good that Tim is very creator minded. It is a wonderful balance, and we very seldom butt heads as long as we know to be strategic about how we present. I think that that is the key to growth.

You have to know your consumer. You have to know your audience. You have to know your marketplace. You have to know how to curate that, and you have to maintain that mentality and control. You can't trust your distributors to do it, your retailers to do it. That's a big reason why we continue to grow retail by putting a taproom in Raleigh and building a restaurant in Asheville; we want to be as direct-to-consumer as possible because it does allow us the wider berth for creativity.

DC: We've tasked readers of this book to really sit down and be honest with themselves when they ask, "What's your differentiator?" There are so many options, but I prohibit one of them being "We're going to make the best beer." If your business model and business plan and financials are built around, "I'm going to move to South Slope, and all of a sudden I'm going to make the best been in town," and that's your hook, then you've got some issues on the way. Shouldn't that be the standard, not the differentiator?

DR: Absolutely. That should be in your head as your hill to climb. That should be that you're setting a standard, that you're going to make all 100-rated beers. You know what I mean? That's not the standard of saying, "I'm going to come in and make beer I like." There's the higher standard than that. Having a standard is very important, and constantly evaluating it is even more important. There is this assumption that everything you put out is good. That's not true.

Every year, your brewery should raise quality standards. Every year, you should sit down and say, "I'm raising the sensory score." I'm changing the sensory system that we use internally, and we're going to make it harder to pass a beer.

I think a good brewery should mandate that a certain amount of beer goes down a drain a year. Honestly, we believe that now. This year – 2019 – is the first time I've put that in place. I've said, "If we get a beer, and we don't like the reaction immediately, we dump."

Quality is so important, but resetting what's good, based upon trends of the industry, is really important, too.

That's why I like having brewers on our staff that actually drink beer. You're not helping me if you're not out there trying stuff. Even stuff you don't like, you damn well better be trying everything, getting a perspective of what consumers consider to be great examples of styles.

I have an amazing staff of super interesting people who are very intelligent. I'm not saying that they're beer nerds. They're not obsessed beer fans, but they are really, really smart. That's something we're looking for in our staff, always, because we want them to contribute to our sensory standards.

DC: As the more business-minded owner in your group, because of the organic and authentic crafting nature of manufacturing beer, cider, spirits, and so on, and as we talked about, the vast majority of breweries in America were opened by the technician, do you feel like sometimes it's taboo to talk about business or focus on financials? That because of our industry's history in organic creativity and growth, the understanding of how to operate successfully as a company away from the brewhouse is something people don't talk about? Jeff Stuffings at Jester King (see Chapter 14), for example, has seemed to nail this balance of organic, amazing creativity and smart business.

DR: Totally. But I think that's becoming less and less every day. It's becoming less taboo. It certainly was, I think, several years ago. It was all about creativity. But now it's about longevity.

Yeah, I think that, for a while there, it was, "The microbrewery is invincible, and creativity is king." I think now intelligence is king. Being aware of consumer taste and what allows you to be a unique person in the marketplace. Jeff is a perfect example of this. You got a niche. He commits to it with reckless abandon, and it allows him to define standards.

I believe us to be some of the best lager producers in the world, IPA producers, and I think we make really great rustic saisons. But Jeff is the kind of mixed culture ale, and he sets the bar. I think his commitment to doing so is a very calculated business decision, just as much as Oxbow has made the same decisions to commit to their product line and not to grow beyond it. They're a name. They're in IPA heaven, and could make IPA and sell boatloads of it.

I have no doubt that they would make incredible IPA, because they are insanely talented people who are really great brewers. But they don't, because they have a core vision, they have a value that they want to try to espouse, and they get to define what makes saison or mix culture ale. That's really, really great.

I think that that is cloaked in creativity. But don't get me wrong – it is immensely predicated on really intentional business calculations. Those guys are wicked smart people. Jeff especially is a really intentional person. I think you never look at it and think, "Why did he do that?" No, every time he makes a decision it makes sense. Even when he gave his management group, his leadership team, some stock ownership last year, that made sense. They're the rustic rural brewery, and it just made sense across the board. It almost played into the story of Jester King.

DC: It reminds me of the book *Moneyball*, where those old-school scouts would say, "I trust my intuition." Then eventually the computer nerds come along – and I think this is not unique to beer and is in every industry going from young to innovation. Sam Calagione often uses Silicon Valley as an example, comparing it to current craft beer, that the guys who first started working there must have done it because they loved it, then things changed. As it innovates and grows and evolves, so does the business acumen of the industry.

DR: As it becomes competitive.

DC: Right. People come in who are a little bit smarter, a little bit better, more imaginative, or a little bit more creative. Naturally, that's just where industry goes. Does it feel like that? Is that where our industry's going?

DR: I think so. Obviously a lot of business professionals see the financial opportunities in craft beverage in general, beer, wine, spirits, kombucha, sodas. Food/entertainment hybrid industries are taking off. There's a ton of opportunity there. You're right. The classically run brewery, most businesspeople almost look down on. They're like,

"You mean that bakery is run by an actual baker? It's not going to be easy for me to come in and steal their pie."

I think that it's certainly become an attractive industry. Fireman's Capital came in from outside and invested immensely in it. You're seeing a lot of outside investment, and a lot of professionals giving up their careers to go do it. I did it as a side hustle for fun, because I wanted to have a fun life that had no business purpose. I never thought I'd make a dollar on it. Like I said, what actually probably propelled us to success in our model was that we did not look businessy at all to the outside world.

But people are smart these days, man. A lot of smart people are attracted to the opportunity to run into a cash-heavy business and dominate demographics of consumer bases. Because creators, brewer-run breweries aren't looking at consumer bases. They're not looking at who the consumers are, what they like, what they want to buy. They're looking at it as, "I want to get my vision out there," always. I think there's immense opportunity. I just know so many of those brewers with business backgrounds and a thirst for just getting into the food/beverage/entertainment business because they were bored with their careers, and they were able to raise $3, $4 million and start five years in to where the rest of everybody had to work to.

There's no reason to be mad about that. There's no reason to think less of those people, necessarily. It doesn't mean they can't make good beer. At the end of the day, like we just said, it's about quality of product. The consumers are going to drink what's good. It doesn't necessarily matter what the story is behind the people and their intentions unless it's told very clearly. Burial has been successful by telling a story. Jester King has been very successful by telling a story. But not everybody has the capacity to do that, or the core value to do so. That's one of our core values.

DC: For the person reading this book, what would your top advice be in 2019, knowing what you know about this market right now? What would you tell them to look out for if they were opening a place today?

DR: Cannabis beer?

DC: Ha, yes.

DR: No. Man, several things. I would tell them, be wary of ego. I think it's the biggest sinking ship in craft beer. Whether your ego is that you have to constantly be different, or whether your ego is you can't share in creativity, or whether your ego is that you can make more beer, or whether your ego is that you have to make the highest price point – whatever it takes to fulfill your ego, we all have it, you need to be aware of it and define it very early on. You need to know that that is a potential blocker for you at all times, and that you may need to step outside of yourself and be objective to make wise business decisions.

The second would be, know where you want to be and try to get there very fast. I knew exactly where I wanted Burial to get to. I wanted us to be 10,000 barrels. I felt that, at 10,000 barrels, we could be a nationally known brewery, but not nationally distributed. We could focus on our local market. We could saturate it in a way that drew people to our retail. The way we look at it is, we make three or four core beers now, for the most part. We distribute those, and that's your introductory card to Burial. It draws you in. You look at the brand, you say, "This is a good fucking beer," but there's not a lot of other options out there for you on the shelf anymore.

A couple years ago, we said we were going to put everything out there. We made a very conscious decision, over the last year or so, to draw that back. Now that we have a wide retail reach, and we're such storytellers, and we believe in the experience, we want to draw people to us. It's the carrot. It's like, "Here we are. Aren't we pretty sweet?"

DC: I call it "billboard distribution," distribution with focus not on a primary funding source, but to bring people into the taproom.

DR: Totally. That enables us to be that size, and still be small. We're small, but we're big enough to get beer into the hands of many, and we're big enough that we have beer available to do events. When we travel, for instance in January, I went to Nashville and brewed a beer with Bearded Iris. We dropped about 200 cases of beer in Nashville, and it was just gone. In a couple days, it was gone off the shelves. Then in February, I came down to Miami, and I did WakeFest and brewed a beer with J. Wake Field. We dropped a couple hundred cases down there.

It's big enough that it allows us to make a difference, but it's not so big that it causes us to lose our niche. It enables us to do just about anything we want. From a creativity point of view, it also allows us to make the things that we want to without hindering getting the beer out there that our audience generally wants.

I knew that, for us, and we're now on a good run of . . . probably 4,000 of those barrels will be retail, maybe 5,000 barrels retail this year, and the other 5,000 out there in the distribution, most of which is in-state distribution, we've grown ourselves. We do direct to the retailer, which is great, because it allows us to control the narrative and relationships.

I knew that's what I wanted to get. I grew as fast as I could. It took me five years to get there. It shouldn't take you five years to get there. You should not do the first two years of the Burial plan. That was stupid. I will tell people that all the time, and people always say, "You should really celebrate those years. It's how you became who you were." They don't know, because they weren't living it every day. It was terrible, and very hard, and a lot of work for very little beer.

DC: I think anyone who suggested opening a taproom today on a one-barrel would know they were setting themselves up for no possible long-term success whatsoever. People don't survive long at that size. You guys are an exception. Somebody who opens like that, they usually would do it because they were undercapitalized. Usually you hear that story about people brewing 24/7 on a two-barrel, one-barrel, or something, that it doesn't work out.

DR: Yeah, you burn out, you limit, you frustrate consumers, and you make beer that is not that good. I think the reason we survived was that we made quick decisions to expand, and we told people that. That was the story. "We're organically growing." "We're going to be there."

The cautionary tale that I speak on panels about – people always ask me about that start because I was a nanobrewery. I always say that it was a terrible decision. I don't think it is smart business for anybody. I'm not saying you need to start at 10,000 barrels, but you need to start with a plan to get the 10,000 barrels in your first two years, whatever your number is. If your number's 50,000, you should start at 5,000, and scale up pretty quick, building your marketplace.

I don't think you should be there on day one. I think it is kind of a two-step process.

Then the third thing is – I don't really know how to put this, but don't be afraid to be small. I really believe in 10,000 barrels. We could make 100,000 barrels and sell it. We have a strong brand. We could make a lot of beer. We could certainly get up into the 20s, 30s, and still self-distro and still be in our realm. But that means a lot more people. That means working people three shifts. That means brewing seven days a week, overnight. It means a lot more equipment.

Expansion is painful, and it hurts. Every time you go through it, everyone gets burned out, and you lose people. There's going to be attrition, because it's just an extremely frustrating struggle when you start to change your workflow significantly. For me, I would go through it once. Because if you had the ideal scenario, you'd open with a decent amount of money. You don't need $3, $4 million – maybe a half million dollars. You start a nice little 10-barrel thing. You do 1,500, 2,000 barrels, and then you try to grow. You expand, or you build your second facility, and you go up to your 10,000 barrels. Then stay there, and make really great beer, and find your hold in the marketplace where you make the best.

Everybody's got to have a differentiator, right? You have to have that thing that makes you special. At Burial, we're really assessing those things right now. I think I know what they are. Those are the things that we're going to continue to improve, and make more of, and focus on. But a lot of breweries just seem to think there's endless runway in front of them, and they're just going to keep making. They're going to satisfy any orders they've got. A) They're not always going to be there, and B) it doesn't allow you to focus on quality. You're just constantly focused on quantity, and that's not good for your brand, long term.

Part V

Getting the Word Out: Branding, Social Media, and Public Relations

As MUCH AS we'd all like to be Kevin Costner in *Field of Dreams*, the truth is that the customer acquisition doesn't just stop at building the brewery of *your* dreams.

In this section we'll explore some tactical keys to branding your businesses, how to utilize social media effectively, and – perhaps most forgotten of all – how to cultivate relationships with journalists and other stakeholders to help get the word out for you.

The journey hasn't ended when you get the brewery open and you make beer. The path to sustained success is just beginning.

Chapter 25

Why Branding Matters

A BREWERY'S BRAND is its window to the world. Much in the same way the theme of this book is to help tackle the "other things" besides making beer that can lead you to be successful, a company's brand and public image can be just as impactful as its product.

And if you don't see any really subpar brewery branding out there, maybe the subpar branding is you. Packaging, branding, logo, the message your brand sends all matter.

Here are some rapid-fire tips to build or to check against your current branding strategy.

1. **Lay out your vision for what your brand looks like.** It's okay to be inspired by other breweries. There is so much branding talent in our industry, we're all naturally going to gravitate to a brewery that speaks loudly to us through their brand and imagery. This is not a directive to rip off their logo, but it's all right to put your own spin on something that inspires you.

   As you start to build the brand identity, it helps to use a few key words to lay out the brand. Here are some examples: Fun, Rebellious, Weird, Clean, Stately, Evil, Angelic – you get the point. Talk with friends and family about what you want your brand to reflect. What's the message you want your brand to send to your community?

   On a second level, how do you plan on utilizing your brand each day to speak to that message? (There's more on social media in the next chapter.)

   Once you have the elevator pitch ready – What does your brand mean to you? What will it convey? What story will it tell? – then you can move to working on the visual piece of your brand.

2. **Understand that the quality of your brand/logo/label/website is a direct reflection of you.** Your logo is the storefront to the world. If you get your crazy cousin to do your logo and treat it as an afterthought, that's what you'll be considered in the eyes of the consumer. We can all recognize terrible labels, logos, and brand identity in this business as quickly as we can pick out the great stuff. Don't fall in the bad pile. Know that your branding matters. Don't consider it a "luxury" expense; consider it an investment with a clear, definitive financial return because you can set yourself apart in your market – and sell more beer – when a brewery can put its best image/brand forward.

3. **Have a logo that speaks to your inspiration.** We toiled and toiled over our logo. We couldn't ever decide on a preconceived font and wanted something truly natural looking that was our own. We danced around a bunch of options but landed on a logo that we felt spoke to us: clean, natural, high quality, classic.

4. **Budget dollars for using a professional for branding.** You've got a lot going on, and branding expense is a wise investment. Some companies pay for someone to do it all. Others just pay for primary and secondary logo work. Depending on your skill set, or if you already have a crystal-clear vision for what you want, you can slide around the investment accordingly. But unless you already come from the professional branding and design world, I would budget some dollars for branding. Between menus, labels, coasters, stickers, T-shirts – you'll need to use them one way or another. Just bite off what you feel you can afford to chew, and when invested with the right branding mind, those dollars will pay you back in spades with your overall brand reputation.

5. **Be sure to ask questions of a branding pro:**
   o Are you familiar with the craft beer space, and what work have you done there?
   o How would you describe the overall feel of your work?
   o What is your fee? (I had quotes ranging from $5,000 to – not joking – $80,000 for the branding of Perfect Plain. We spent much closer to the former. I am in no way suggesting that money is not an object. You can get quality of work for a fairly reasonable price.)
   o Do you have any conflicts I should know about, like doing work for neighborhood breweries? (Outside of quality work and beer

perfectplain
Perfect Plain Brewing Co.   •••

View Insights   Promote

 Liked by **twobirdsstreetfood** and **168 others**

experience, the reason we ultimately decided to hire the woman who did our branding for us to start, Veronique Zayas of Hatchmark Studio, was because she told me up front that she and her husband were planning on opening a brewery in town one day, so I knew it *could* become a conflict down the road. The fact that she volunteered that information meant she was honest and ethical about her business and signaled to me I could trust her.)

o What would it cost do additional design like crowler labels, or can labels down the road? (It's good to negotiate pricing on the potential additional work up front.)

Chapter 26

Tips for Improving Your Social Media Presence

DESPITE A DECADE spent in the more traditional – some might say archaic – advertising platform of the print newspaper, the lion's share of our marketing budget is used on the digital and social media platforms of Facebook and Instagram.

I love the hard work journalists do to deliver the news and be our city's watchdog. However, we know that our target market is best found not through a full-page print advertisement, but through digital platforms. All of our ad dollars in 18 months – other than a few "thank you" award ads here and there – have been through the creation of our own art and video, Facebook, Instagram, and some subtle digital targeting during tourist season.

The largest marketing expense we've taken on so far was hiring the best videographer team in our city, Calliope Films, to make 45- to 60-second spots to use not for television but for social media.

The vast majority of the time we aren't paying anything; we're just cultivating the best social media presence we can without using any dollars. It's the most effective way to reach our target audience, and our brewery business model – pretty tanks, pretty beers, outside-the-box creative processes – is tailor-made to put on display.

Telling brewery owners to have good social media isn't exactly a novel idea, but you'd be surprised how many breweries are doing it wrong. Or not doing it at all. I won't go into too deep a technical dive here because there is a bevy of resources online that can help you learn the technical side of how to post, what to post, that 8–9 a.m. and 8–9 p.m. Monday–Thursday are the best times to post, and so on.

perfectplain
Perfect Plain Brewing Co.

View Insights   Promote

Liked by **thomas3times** and **734 others**

perfectplain We are forever grateful for being so welcomed as a part of our great community.

So today, we announce our new commitment to the vibrancy of Downtown Pensacola: The Grainhouse and City Garden at Perfect Plain.

The Grainhouse, a former feed and seed warehouse in the early 1900s, will become our barrel room and event rental space. We will begin taking reservations soon.

Hire staff that understands it. It's an asset to have as many people on the team as possible who understand and use social media well. It's important enough to me, in fact, that I ask every interview candidate about it, even if they aren't in charge of our accounts. What about when a celebrity walks in to try our beer, or that great moment when a dog walks in with our Perfect Plain collar on? Will that bartender know that's a great potential post down the road? Will they know to ask the dog's owners whether they have an Instagram account that we can tag the post in? Do they know how to stage a pretty photo with the sun over their shoulder and not blindingly arranged into the sun?

perfectplain
Perfect Plain Brewing Co.

View Insights   Promote

Liked by **thomas3times** and **547 others**

I'll take as much social media expertise and knowledge as I can get. It's that important to me. If someone has video or graphic design talent on your staff, use it! Creating quality content matters very much and it is one of the most cost-effective ways for any brewery to set itself apart in its market.

High-quality photos and video. Social media posts and photos speak volumes to your consumers. Junky, blurry photos send the unintended message that you really don't care about your product. This is probably the most common mistake that breweries make on

Photo

perfectplain
Perfect Plain Brewing Co.

View Insights   Promote

Liked by **thomas3times** and **144 others**

social media. While plenty can be accomplished even with today's smart phones, it doesn't serve your business to post random photos with no real thought of poignancy or timing to them. If you're not comfortable doing your own photography or assigning someone on staff to do it, there is certainly a litany of professional photographers in your area that could be hired for an afternoon for a reasonable cost (or beer trade).

Before you post anything, ask yourself: What are you trying to accomplish? It's not a trick question. Are you releasing a new beer? Are you announcing an event? Are you highlighting work with a community nonprofit? Putting a little bit of thought into your posts will go a long way with your followers.

Social Media 202: Fewer Coupons, More Immersive Brewery Experience

Yet again, breweries have the distinct advantage that we make our quality product with our own hands. There are so many opportunities

to narrate that story with your fans. Photos of mashing in. Photos of adding hops in the kettle. Photos of putting that beautiful liquid into a beautiful barrel. Think about all those opportunities to share your day to day experience with your guests.

What would they like to know? That you are handcrafting their beer with care and love. That you take steps to create high-quality product. They like seeing those crazy ingredients take a slow-motion dive into the wort. All of this is great social media content that can set you apart and let people in on the experience.

The same goes for impactful events at your place. Take a photo of a busy taproom and say thank you in a heartfelt way on social media the next day. It matters to your customers.

It's perfectly okay to mention drink specials, happy hours, or that sort of thing. Just be tactful in how you do it. Don't simply take a picture of a coupon you made on your computer. If it's a crowler special, for example, get a sharp, clean photo of someone filling one up. Take it to the beach or on a hike somewhere with a pretty backdrop. You'll get the discount message across in a much prettier way.

Concentrate on showing fewer coupons and offer more prettiness that happens to include something about a special in the caption.

The Caption Is Just as Valuable

Pay attention to your caption and messaging. Again, what is the desired outcome for the viewer? Make sure your grammar is correct, it's not written in all caps or something similarly obnoxious (unless it's a joke).

Ask yourself what you are trying to get the consumer to do, and make sure the message is tailored to that desired outcome.

For example, we like posting our most beautiful drink photos on Fridays because we know *everyone* needs a drink by Friday. The primary message will be what we did to make this pretty drink you see. That's the focus of the messaging. We may have live music going on to, so while we don't need just a random photo of a guy with a

perfectplain   •••

View Insights   Promote

Liked by **reedodeneal** and **132 others**

guitar, we can subtly mention live music, drink specials, and so near the end of the caption so we don't appear to be pushing a hard sales-only pitch. Rather than feeling like you're only interested in selling them something, customers want interesting content that tells them something about the experience they'll get from visiting your establishment.

perfectplain
Tatooine

...

View Insights   Promote

Liked by **reedodeneal** and **129 others**

How Often Should You Post?

I'm not sure what the right answer is here, but in my experience, I feel that the newer the brewery, the more often you should post. We have been attempting to post on social platforms once a day since we opened, though we are more likely to miss a day than we are ever to post twice in a day.

This chapter presents some of our Instagram posts over the past year. We aim for a mix of messages used conscientiously, from beer and brewing imagery, to funny stuff, to breaking news on an expansion. Be mindful of the entire journey you are creating with your social media, not just day-to-day obligations to post.

perfectplain
Denver, Colorado

View Insights   Promote

Liked by **reedodeneal** and **677 others**

Chapter 27

How to Get the Local Media on Your Side

Media coverage for a brewery is often treated like a spare tire. You only care about it when you need it.

After more than a decade as a journalist, I've seen both sides of this dilemma. Fortunately, living as a journalist first has prepared me to know what businesses should do to optimize their chances at getting the best kind of exposure out there: free, objective exposure.

This may be outdated, but when I was in the business mid-2010s we used a common metric that objective news coverage about an event or a business was worth **2.6 times** more than a paid advertisement. Think about your own media consumption. Do you give more credence to an ad you see about a brewery or when CraftBeer.com does an article on the same brewery?

Earned media is valuable in so many ways.

So, what helps a business get exposure, and what makes it as likely as possible that a journalist will take on your story? We are grateful for our local media, the *Pensacola News Journal*, WEAR3-TV, Ballinger Publishing, and the *Independent Weekly*, who have all been gracious with their time and coverage of our company and our events.

Be aware, however, that there is no guarantee of coverage just because you send a journalist or blogger an e-mail. Don't be mad if they don't respond. They get zillions of e-mails just like yours.

We think that our insider industry knowledge has helped garner more coverage, and I'm passing that knowledge on to you today. Here are my suggested ways to maximize your chances of getting more coverage than most.

1. **Don't call only when you need something.** This is the classic – and most common – mistake of every small business. They contact the newspapers, websites, and TV stations a week or two out from their big event, and then they can't understand why the media outlet didn't cover it. Did you already have a relationship with them? Does the media trust you? Do you reach out any other time outside of when you want them to cover something for you? It's no different than any other relationship. If you cultivate it, and mind it, you will benefit. Call up your local newspaper and sponsor a happy hour for their staff – *without asking for anything in return.* Let them know who you are and the type of operation you run. If you can cultivate the relationship effectively, it will pay off in the long run.

2. **Don't cry wolf.** Every business thinks that every event it ever puts on must be the most important event in the city. That's not the truth. Having a good gauge of the type of events you should and shouldn't pitch to local media outlets can prove quite valuable. Ask yourself: What's the "hook?" What makes this "news?"

   A beer special isn't news. A happy hour isn't news. A new piece of equipment in your brewery isn't news. I can't even count how many soccer or baseball coaches called me during my days as a journalist to explain how they were coaching in the biggest middle school recreational soccer league game of all time and how we just *had* to cover it.

   Newsworthy occurrences may be something like conducting the first "Beer Mile" in your city's history. Or perhaps it's the big check presentation you are doing for the charity you have supported all year long. Or it's that funky or goofy event like giving everyone $2 beers if they were willing to lock up their smart phone in a box for two hours. See the difference between this and a beer special? There's a news hook. The media is a business, too, and their business is clicks and views. That's why you need to pitch something compelling that people who aren't your parents or family members would actually want to read about.

   Make sure you come up with those ideas, but also be sure to use discretion when you are making a pitch to the media. If you call every week just because of your happy hour, reporters – who happen to be regular human beings like you and me – will begin to tune you out. Save your bullets for the best events so the media knows that when you call, it's not just you being desperate for free publicity.

Try to step out of your role and use this litmus test: If I didn't own or care about this brewery, what would be cool enough for me to want to click on it?

3. **Understand what the media wants and needs.** If you are pitching a story on that new brewery expansion, make sure you have something to provide the media; photos, a press release, or at a minimum some bullet points and the Five Ws (Who, What, When, Where, Why) in e-mail form. So often companies will be lackadaisical and think the media's job is to gather all that. Resources in journalism have never been scarcer. This is not the 1980s. All media is more short-staffed than ever, and anything you can do to make their job easier only increases your chances for exposure and coverage. Be proactive. Take professional (not cell phone) photos and send them in. Provide a couple of quotes in your entry about the event. Even if your local media can't cover your event the day it happens, take photos and send them in that evening. They may still be interested in posting a photo gallery or covering the event after the fact.

4. **Be thoughtful.** There's so much stress involved in the media business that a cold beer is powerful. That need ultimately brought me from that world to this one as I fell in love with craft beer as a journalist. All those deadline Saturdays filing a late game story from those Atlantic Coast Conference or Southeastern Conference press boxes with only seconds to spare caused plenty of stress. When my work was done, my goal was to hit the town looking for the best craft beer experience, and so many of those taproom experiences helped build our vision for Perfect Plain. I wanted to take all those great things I saw about breweries and move them to Pensacola. There are plenty more writers like me who enjoy a beer. Send a handwritten note, a T-shirt, and a few free beer cards. This costs you next to nothing, and maybe the journalist will pick up your call next time.

Part VI

Capturing the Heart of Your Brewery: How to Love Your Community

THE VAST NUMBER of breweries in the United States before Prohibition and the meteoric rise of breweries today have at least one common thread: their neighbors and their communities, both large and small, became their foundation.

Without community support, and our human fulfilment as consumers to support local businesses and business owners, this growth would never happen.

I believe we owe our local communities more than beer specials. Can you truly be a community brewery when all you are doing is accepting business from that community? We all owe it to the locals to pay that support forward and become part of the fabric of the communities we are in.

We discuss our experiences as well as share best practices with Matt Stevens of the incredibly giving Creature Comforts Brewing in Athens, Georgia.

Chapter 28

Love Your Community, and It Will Love You Back

Community is part of our fabric. It's part of our company mission statement: "To create incredible experiences that make our beer, our brewery, and our hometown, Pensacola, unforgettable."

Before you roll your eyes and mumble to yourself that "we love our community!" is part of the small business cliché starter kit, we go out of our way to make our charitable work impactful and widespread in an area of Florida that can use it in so many ways.

My two favorite compliments we get at Perfect Plain are:

1. *"This taproom reminds me of a place in Denver/Portland/San Diego/ Asheville."* I love that because it's exactly what we hoped to accomplish with our taproom.
2. When someone I don't know e-mails and says, *"Since you guys are so big in helping the community . . ."* The fact that the word is out in our city among strangers that we're here to build our city up is both intentional on our part and one of the most rewarding parts of owning this company.

It's not just a tagline on our business card. We live it each day. It's part of our fabric.

At Perfect Plain, we have one condition to our charitable giving: All dollars must stay local. If a national organization is doing a local fundraiser but they plan to send those dollars to Orlando or Tampa, we won't do it. Our charity is solely focused on building up our community. I strongly suggest having a similar policy.

Creature Comforts in Athens, Georgia, is a prime example. They started a nonprofit arm, Get Comfortable, and they donate to all kinds of worthy causes and have dedicated taproom revenues on specific nights. They have homed in and refined their work in this area as they have grown, and you'll hear from the head of that effort, Matt Stevens, in the next chapter.

Early on in a startup business, it can be scary to commit to financial obligations, charitable or otherwise. However, there are so many ways to handle this that is helpful to your community.

- Discounted rental space and/or beer for holding events at the brewery
- Keg/beer/merchandise donations for auction items at charity fundraisers
- Partnering with a nonprofit or cause to host a fundraiser at your location (We recently hosted a fundraiser for Stephen Grogan, a young local police officer battling brain cancer with a wife and two children. The event was packed, and we helped raise $11,000 for the Grogan family on one Wednesday night.)

- Pouring beer at a charitable event with a portion of the proceeds going back to the charity
- A portion of beer sales going to a charity during an event they hold at the brewery
- Partner with a local cause for a bottle release (We designed a collaboration beer with Idyll Hounds Brewing Co. in Santa Rosa Beach, Florida, partnering with our local Gulfarium's sea turtle initiative.)

Let me wax a little on a bigger picture market behavior in craft beer. Our breweries and taprooms are a direct beneficiary of the "buy local" emergence across several industries in our nation. Beer is not alone in this movement. We are part of something bigger. Most of us are willing to spend a few extra dollars to get that immersive experience. That beer that was made in our city. Or that tank over there in the corner.

If you combine our country's increased desire to live like a local and support local with the emergence of information at our fingertips, it makes us empowered to find the best beer, the best Mexican food, the best anything in any city on the planet in a matter of seconds.

In the 1970s and 1980s, our parents would take us to Chili's or TGI Friday's during a vacation because all they had to rely on to find great local food was probably a AAA TripTik and a paper map.

The abundance of information from websites, company reviews, and rankings have changed the game and given the buy-local movement its strong engine.

If you care about craft beer enough at any level to pick up this book, there's a good chance that when you take a trip to New York City your goal isn't to hit Olive Garden in Times Square (in spite of delicious breadsticks). You want that same immersive and authentic experience that attracts us to brewery taprooms. It's the primary reason that chain restaurants are downsizing now.

I wanted to set that stage because it's important to understand that even though I believe this to be true, I also believe that all small local business owners should know that they aren't owed anything. Because I know a few small business owners who think that, too.

Just because you open a local business doesn't guarantee that you'll get local business. There are competitors for the same local (and potentially tourist) dollars. In this taproom-focused model, that competition extends to local bars as well as breweries. Local businesses shut down every day.

We discussed earlier how important it is to differentiate your brewery or bar to achieve success. In addition, I believe that being proactive about your position in the community is also vital.

For all the grief that millennials take in the public realm, I believe we are more willing to follow our hearts to do the right thing. It's not that previous generations refused to donate to a charity night or help nonprofits. But I think older generations wanted to see a clearer picture of their return on investment.

Our generation appears more likely to do what our heart tells us is the right thing to do, even if that means it doesn't help our business directly or it loses us revenue.

The most common giving we do is donating $1 per beer on a particular night to different charitable causes around our city. I don't run an ROI analysis on whether it's good for business to do this. It's the right thing to do, and you know what? It might bring in a lot of people who haven't been to our place. It probably touches enough hearts to build some great community advocates for our company and our brand. (Remember those e-mails from strangers about our community impact?) Those are things that no spreadsheet can track, and no survey can reveal.

This concept also means having the owners or leaders take an active role in the community when possible. Realtors and attorneys are quite good at this. After all, they require relationships to succeed. It's even harder for them; breweries don't require relationships, just a strong reputation and simple thirst.

It's the reason many lawyers and realtors are involved in rotary clubs, nonprofit boards, committees, neighborhood cleanups, and more. Don't wait for people to e-mail you or come to your taproom to impact your community. Be proactive.

Being active still means there is no immediate and clear ROI. You can't be in it for the ROI – it's not why I dedicate the time to these causes. But I can't even count how many different opportunities I've had on the nonprofit boards where someone saw me at a meeting and asked me about holding a table for their birthday party. Or a chance to throw a charity event for one of the boards I'm on. So even if you don't care about the full heart and good karma that comes with being a great community advocate, being out there means people are thinking about you and your business. Find some worthy cause you're passionate about and get involved.

I believe that when we impact our community in a positive way without the promise of a direct return, the return comes in gratitude and full hearts for your organization. That's what you can count on.

Building a reputation not just as a great place for beer, but a great place for community, and a great place that supports its city, is an incredible feeling for the owner, the staff, and the whole organization.

Chapter Homework

Identify a plan for community activism and charitable giving. This will most certainly change over time. Early on, don't focus on a dollar amount, just concentrate on tactics you would like to implement. Even better, perhaps find one or several worthy causes, or even a sector of causes (environment, children, cancer treatment, etc.) that you care most about. As we established Perfect Plain, we were able to offer more to more organizations. The big win here is that not only are you doing something great for your community and enjoying that fulfillment, but there's a great chance you are also introducing your brewery to people who have would not have experienced it otherwise. You get a chance to bring in first-time customers and have them leave feeling great about your company.

Chapter 29

Community Q&A: Creature Comforts Brewing Co.'s Matt Stevens

MATT STEVENS IS the Director of Community and Culture at Creature Comforts Brewing Co. in Athens, Georgia, one of the fastest-growing breweries in the Southeast. What's just as impressive as their growth is the way CCBC has integrated itself into the fabric of its hometown.

We all know that this community relationship is vital. And while most breweries aren't at the size of Creature Comforts, there's a lot to learn conceptually about the way CCBC has become known for its good deeds in Athens, and more recently, making impacts in communities where it serves its product regionally.

So much so, in fact, that it hired Stevens, who brings more than a decade of nonprofit and university-based work to their team. He is in charge of the company's community impact programming that includes Get Comfortable, Get Artistic, Get Neighborly, and Brew for One.

In this Q&A, Stevens explains what works well in community impact for CCBC, the importance and impact of that relationship with your hometown, and what any brewery can do – regardless of size – to help grow its heart for its community.

D.C. Reeves: Creature Comforts does such a great job of structuring and galvanizing their community efforts, but for a brewery not at that level yet, to be able to dedicate staff to this cause, what are two or three things any brewery can do to build their relationship with the community?

Matt Stevens: Great question. Well, if I have any advice it's always start as quickly as possible, whatever it is. As far as the low-hanging fruit, I mean, good grief, I think the pub is really the crossroads of humanity and kind of always has been. So, the space itself is really in many ways where Creature Comforts started leveraging the company to give back.

So, we have a great location, we're right in downtown, but we were able to say, "Gosh, the Athens Farmer's Market (AFM) meets in downtown when it's in season." But not really in an ideal situation. And it was a very easy conversation to the AFM just to say, "Hey, moving forward, would y'all be interested in setting up at Creature Comforts for no charge?" For them it was a huge win because one, instead of paying the city to set up, they just got to do it for free. That was a cool way to leverage our space. Two, it's also paid off as far as our brewers developing relationships with all these local farms since we now do a beer series where we're sourcing a lot of these ingredients, raspberries, peaches, whatever, from the local farms. So that's just kind of a side benefit.

But the other cool thing was we were able to, and we still do this today, if you come in on market day, you can buy anything at Creature Comforts and we'll give you tokens to the farmer's market. You just walk outside, and you exchange your tokens for tomatoes or a baguette or whatever. And Creature just picks up the bill. We just kind of tally all the tokens at the end of every market day and we distribute our money to those local farms. So, it was kind of a cool way just to support local farmers. It's an investment, but it's a pretty easy one to get on its feet.

So anyway, beyond just the farmer's market, leveraging our space. Chances are in every single community where there's a brewery there is a vibrant nonprofit community meeting all these various social service needs. And those agencies have annual or biannual fundraisers. I mean that's how a lot of their development is happening and how they're continuing to be the nonprofit that they are. That's been another cool way is we've just been able to say to nonprofits, "Hey, if you want to do your fundraiser at Creature, just let us know." And once again, free of charge. We allow them to throw their annual event in what I would say is a pretty cool space. Every now and again we're able to obviously throw in beer as well. And so the beer sales at night are also fundraising for the agency. So that's just another idea, every brewery, probably every taproom probably has a space that can be leveraged in a lot of cool ways to serve the community around it.

DC: **What do you guys feel like you've learned through the process? Let's just say I'm starting a brewery and I have no value consideration for whether I want to help the community or not. Give me your elevator pitch or sales pitch to convince me, this guy or gal who started a brewery – what is your value argument for doing this, even for somebody who may not care about it morally or spiritually or otherwise? Talk about that side of it too. What value could that bring to a business?**

MS: I mean, one of the things that we say all the time is that good companies are good neighbors. They have a plan to support the city they love. And I think the operative word there is "plan." It's not when it occurs to us –we'd like to cut a check to something. And there's nothing wrong with that, but I think the truly great companies of the world have a plan to support those around them. So, a little quick context and then I'll answer your question. One of the great assignments I would give them right when I came into this position was before you activate any new programming that we figure out what great companies do on the community impact side, like the companies that are very famous for leveraging their brand.

I was just cold-calling companies, buying lunch, bringing beer and saying, "I only need about 30 minutes of your time, but I have three questions for you." And man, with that sort of pitch for whatever it's worth, these great companies have been incredibly generous with their time and resources. I spent an entire day at Googleplex, Google's headquarters out in San Francisco. I spent an entire day at Slack, and at Ramsey Solutions and at MailChimp and at Patagonia and others. Once again, good companies really are good neighbors, they tend to be the very types that want to open up their playbook and share with other companies that are trying to bring to life the same value system they have, they say this is how we figured it out here at Google and I come home and say here's what we're going to do at Creature.

But in a lot of cases we've been able to kind of contextualize and scale some version of what these great companies are doing. So being a student of other great industries, I've come to think of it as a kind of cultural reconnaissance. That has been a huge inspiration for a lot of what we have launched here. So that's just some context.

So, to your point, Google is your friend (and I'm not talking about Google the company, but Google the function on your computer). It's easy to find the types of information that suggest that today's consumers and especially the upcoming generation of millennials are the types who very much care not only about ethically sourced coffee and produce or whatever. They hear about good products that are done responsibly. But increasingly beyond just the product, today's consumer is more and more interested in supporting companies that they believe in. And so even if you're just bottom-line focused, orienting your business around a kind of a corporate philanthropic position is going to serve you well. In my opinion that's not why you do it, but maybe it is.

DC: Maybe what's different with your dad's or granddad's situation versus ours is I think companies with younger leadership now are willing to take that blind chance of like, "Yes, I'm sending this dollar out the door to support a great thing in our community and no, I don't know what the ROI on it is. But I do know that I just trust that it's the right thing to do and that support will turn around and come back to me in some fashion, I guess?

MS: Yeah. Absolutely, but I guess I would also throw in a word of caution. If, for lack of a better phrase, if your intentions aren't pure what I would also say is two things. One is that there is a distinction between being seen doing good and doing good to be seen. And I would further argue that people today, because we just consume so much media, that's a neutral idea. But I think we're very, very astute as consumers to the authenticity or the integrity of a message and we're very suspicious. Bottom line, I think we know bullshit when we see it. I really do. But I also think we know integrity when we see it as well. And you've used the most successful example, and this is just something I made up, but it's something I call the "Bono effect."

I mean, the reason that 15-year-old Matt Stevens cared about Make Poverty History or UNICEF or Amnesty International, any of the other incredible causes that Bono champions is because he was very, very comfortable being seen doing good. And I guess I call it the Bono effect because people gathered around U2 because they wrote great pop songs. But once upon a time you realize, "Well you know what, they're coming for the music. But while I have their attention, I can say, hey, okay, while you're looking at me, look over here. Did you know that, fill in the blank, or here's an opportunity to take a step while you're here today to engage in this incredible organization?"

He knew that they came for the music, and he could engage certain percentages of the people who took them seriously to get them engaged in world or local affairs or whatever.

And I feel like any brewery, or any company for that matter, has the same opportunity. They can enact the Bono effect because of the same idea, people will come to Creature Comforts and to other breweries because you have excellent beer, you have this engaging environment, and so on. So, while they're there, it comes with a beer. You have an opportunity to kind of say, "Hey, look over here," and perhaps engage. And back to the original idea, maybe he has totally fooled me, but after paying attention to him for most of my life, I think there's incredible integrity and a very genuine approach that he has taken. But effectively he's just very comfortable being seen doing good. And I don't think he's doing good just to be seen. And people can tell the difference.

DC: And actually, maybe that's a great kind of second-level point with this question. As you said, we're in an all-sorts-of-communication kind of world – how do you strike that balance of wanting to turn doing a good thing and having a good heart for the community and not trivializing it or overblowing it? Like every time you give $1 to anybody, you Instagram about it. Do you feel like there's a balance or do you think it's okay to say, "Here's all the good that we're doing"? How about the communication piece of the good work a brewery does?

MS: Great question. I think there is a balance, but part of it is I don't think Creature Comforts, or whatever the brand is, should make themselves the hero because in many ways they're not. If you look at our Get Comfortable program as just one example, Creature's not the hero, Creature is just like the mirror or the guide or there's a lot of different analogies you can use. We're the ones who are trying to mobilize dollars, manpower, awareness, whatever to who we think the heroes are, which are these nonprofits, which are the people in the trenches doing the work. We're just trying to be the wind in the sails of great work happening. So, whether it's social media or PR or whatever, if we're positioning ourselves as, "Look how great we are," we're making ourselves the hero and that's not going to be effective.

But I do think standing up to say, "Here's something we did, this is why we did it and this is why you should know about the impact and let us tell you part of their story and why they're the stars and you should know about them." And hey, if you come in, part of what you're spending is going to be gone to support this. But we're not making ourselves the hero. And I think that's an important piece of the equation.

DC: What other recommendations do you have for breweries looking to do good with their new or soon-to-be new platform in their community?

MS: Here's a great recommendation and this one probably translates almost anywhere. For any given community there might be a better resource, but this is at least a good thing to get off the starting block. You say, "Okay, I want to do something great. I want to make sure any impact I'm trying to make is not already happening and I want to make sure that if we're not going to go the community route, maybe I'm going to go more the college route." Like actually we care about cancer research or we care about youth intervention or a specific cause, that's fine too, but know whatever your intended impact is before you activate anything. The recommendation I would say is reach out to United Way.

As you can see, they're one of our advisory committee members. United Way has 1,800 chapters around the world, so chances are there is a United Way in your community. They're the ones who kind of are collecting a lot of this needs assessment data. They're the ones who are interpreting the data. They're the ones who are making recommendations to city officials. I mean they're the ones cutting checks to local nonprofits. So, I would say that's pretty easy and pretty transferable. Reach out to your local United Way chapter and say, "Hey, we're a business. We want to do something great with our company. Once again, can I buy you lunch and beer and ask you a few questions?"

212 Capturing the Heart of Your Brewery: How to Love Your Community

I promise you any United Way in the world would say we would love to talk to you. Because the last thing any United Way wants is, again, another solution championed by someone that might not be a particularly important solution or it might be a solution that would just be a duplication of other great work happening. So, I think a partnership like that or with your local community foundation, there's a lot of kind of transferable equivalents but that is a great first conversation to have.

DC: How do you engage and involve your own employees in the community, the things that you're doing, and make them not only a part of it, but excited to be a part of the good deeds you do?

Once again, authenticity I think is a big part of that equation that you're going to be trying to invite your employee base to participate in kind of a community-minded thing. I do think your employees will also know if your heart is true. So that has to be authentic, of course. But as far as the playbook, the nuts and bolts, making serving simple – at Creature Comforts this year again we had 10 local nonprofit agencies that were calling our Get Comfortable partners.

There's kind of two ways that we engage. One is that throughout the year we'll create opportunities for a nonprofit agency to come on site and try to bring to life the work they do and the community within the walls of our brewery. And that's for the benefit or the engagement of our customers, but also of our staff. So just picture you walk in one day, oh there's an organization and they have their banners and flags on a table and a lot of their employees or volunteers wearing shirts.

When you can just say, "Hey, what are you all about?" Of course, at some point throughout the night we'll get on the mic and say, "Hey, tonight in the house, if you haven't noticed, we have our firms from (blank) here, they're a Get Comfortable partner. Here's the one-liner of what they do in our city. If you don't know about them, just go have a beer with them really quick or just go say hello or whatever." But also, for example, we'll help that nonprofit assemble kit projects that they disperse to their clients. And so we'll set up a station where you kind of do a round robin and you grab a bag and fill with one of those, two of those, one of those, things like local bus passes and shampoo perhaps, and deodorant or feminine hygiene products or whatever.

So, it's kind of cool because our customers in 60 seconds can create a kit project that the nonprofit will then turn around and hand off to their clients. But then the other kind of piece is our customer says, "Wow, I didn't really think about if you're serving the homeless population that yeah, gosh, how do they get around? How do they even take advantage of this nonprofit if they have to walk seven miles outside of town to get there? Oh, well these bus passes are a big part of their livelihood. Never even thought about that." So, some of that empathy should be generated through that moment as well. So that's one way we engage partners is we have the agencies themselves come onsite and help tell their story and engage in that way.

Second, we have an easy way to engage our staff through a website signup page with information about the nonprofit, the event, and so on. So, if you want to you can reach out directly to the volunteer coordinator to understand, "Wait, I want to serve, but how is this going to work?" you can see their information there.

Through those two avenues, we try and make it very simple for our staff to go out and serve with these partners. I think that's two of the ways that we have tried to lower the bar as much as possible to make serving the city we love as simple as possible for our staff.

Appendix 1
Perfect Plain Brewing Co.: Manage Up Employee Questionnaire

Name: _____

Position:_____

PPBC employment start date: _____

Hometown:_____

A couple of sentences about your family:

_____

_____

_____

What is your education level? Where did you obtain your education from?

_____

_____

_____

What is your work experience? Number of years in your field? Any other work or unique experience you're bringing to the PPBC team?

_____

_____

_____

Do you have any certifications?

_____

_____

_____

Have you received any awards/honors?

_____

_____

_____

Do you volunteer in the community, schools, nonprofits?

_____

_____

_____

Hobbies:

_____
_____
_____

Favorite food/snack/local restaurant:

_____
_____
_____

Favorite beer (besides ours!)/cocktail/glass of wine/local bar:

_____
_____
_____

Favorite sport/team:

_____
_____

What one book would you want on a deserted island?

_____

Which fictional TV or movie cast would you want to have a beer with and why?

_____

Is there anything else you'd like someone to know about you?

_____
_____
_____
_____
_____
_____

Appendix 2
Perfect Plain Brewing Co.: New Hire Checklist

Name: _____ Position: _____Date: _____

RECRUITMENT	**Date Completed**

☐ Complete Application for Employment Received _____

   ☐ Equal Opportunity Employer Applicant's Statement

   ☐ Employee Background Investigation Authorization

   ☐ Drug Testing Consent, Release, and Acknowledgment Form

   ☐ Worker's Compensation Policy Acknowledgment Form

   ☐ Authorization for Limited Use or Disclosure of Medical Info

☐ Resume and Cover Letter Received _____

☐ Job Description Signed _____

☐ Standards of Behavior Signed _____

☐ First Interview (DC) _____

☐ Second Interview (BB/Nate/Reed) _____

☐ Peer Interview (Supervisor to schedule peers) _____

☐ Reference Checks _____

☐ Background/Credit Checks _____

☐ Send/Receive Signed Offer Letter _____

INTERNAL

☐ Schedule Bev Law Class _____

☐ Schedule 30-Day/90-Day/Midyear/ _____
End Year Evals

☐ Add Birthday to Calendar _____

☐ Schedule Training _____

☐ Add Employee to Sling Schedule _____

☐ Add Employee to Square POS/Payroll _____

TRAINING DAY 1

ORIENTATION

The PPBC Culture

☐ Issue Copy of Standards of Behavior _____

☐ Discuss Mission/Vision/Values/Standards of _____
Behavior

☐ Our Story _____

☐ Beer by Us _____

☐ Meet Managers and Coworkers _____

☐ Facility Tour _____

☐ Create Employee Folder _____

☐ Complete New Hire Paperwork _____

☐ Fill out I-9

☐ Fill out W-4

☐ Manage Up Personal Information Sheet _____

☐ Receipt for Company Property Form (if _____
applicable)

☐ Issue Employee Handbook and Discuss
Expectations _____

☐ Discuss All PPBC Employee Handbook
Policies _____

☐ Sign Employee Handbook Acknowledgment _____

TRAINING DAY 2

BEER SCHOOL

☐ How We Make Beer: The brewing process at
PPBC _____

☐ Beer Style Guide: An overview of the
official BJCP style guide and how our beers can
relate to this _____

☐ Experiencing Perfect Plain's Beer: A deep
dive into each beer that PPBC offers that
details the story, process, ingredients, and presentation for each _____

Standard Operating Procedures – Back of House

Cellaring Procedures _____

☐ Changing Kegs

☐ Changing Service Tanks

☐ Cold Room Organization

☐ Fermentation Vessel Crashing

☐ Beer Sample Collecting

Cleaning Procedures _____

   ☐ Cellar Floors

   ☐ Draft Beer Lines

   ☐ Kegs

   ☐ Raw Goods Storage

Raw Materials Handling Procedures   _____

    ☐ Raw Materials Delivery

    ☐ Yeast Storage

    ☐ Hop Storage

    ☐ Grain Storage

Equipment Maintenance Procedures   _____

    ☐ Equipment Delivery

    ☐ Equipment Malfunctions

Crowler Training   _____

Wine School   _____

TRAINING DAY 3

☐ Beverage Law/Sexual Harassment/Food   _____
Service Training

☐ All other product training   _____

TRAINING DAY 4

Standard Operating Procedures: Front of House

☐ Square POS System   _____

    ☐ Money, Checkout, Security

    ☐ Gift Cards

    ☐ Promos/Comps/Voids

    ☐ Food Truck Orders

☐ Opening and Closing Duties   _____

    ☐ Bar Setup and Breakdown

    ☐ Bar Cleanliness

    ☐ Bar Equipment Instructions/Maintenance

    ☐ Glassware Storage/Polishing/Breakage

    ☐ Setting the Music

    ☐ Handling the AV

    ☐ Setting the Thermostat

    ☐ Setting the Lighting

    ☐ Floor Chart

    ☐ Menu Checks/Printing

    ☐ Stocking Product Behind the Bar and Par Levels

    ☐ Stocking Dry Goods Behind the Bar and Par Levels

    ☐ Setting up Games

☐ Running Sidework During Service Hours   _____

☐ Bathroom Checks

☐ Inside Bussing/Cleaning

☐ Outside Bussing/Cleaning

☐ Dishes

☐ Weekly/Monthly/Quarterly Cleaning   _____
Assignments

☐ Handling Merchandise _____

☐ Handling Lost Credit Card _____

☐ Customer Survey Collection _____

☐ Employee and Customer Injury/Accident _____

☐ Selling a Flight _____

☐ Handling Customers _____

    ☐ Complaints

    ☐ Children

    ☐ Assisting the Disabled

☐ Receiving FoH Orders _____

☐ Founder's Club _____

☐ Answering the Phone _____

☐ Directions to PPBC _____

☐ Fielding Inquiries to the Correct Staff Members _____

TRAINING DAY 5

SERVICE

☐ PPBC Steps of Service _____

☐ Establishing Guest Relations for Future Sales _____

☐ Role Playing _____

☐ First Day Behind the Bar _____

TRAINING DAY 6

☐ Open/Close on-the-Job Training _____

☐ Complete All SOPs with MOD Assistance _____

TRAINING DAY 7

☐ Open/Close on-the-Job Training   _____

☐ Complete all SOPs without MOD assistance   _____

☐ Final Exam   _____

Long-Term Training

☐ Beverage Law Class Completed   _____

☐ Brew Day Completed   _____

Appendix 3
Core Values and Standards of Behavior

Mission

To create incredible experiences that make our beer, our brewery, and our hometown, Pensacola, unforgettable.

Vision

To set the standard for the brewery experiences in the United States with exemplary product, atmosphere, quality, and customer service.

Core Values

We believe that our core values accurately communicate the things that drive us as an organization. As members of Perfect Plain Brewing Company, we are expected to live the values and embrace the spirit of our behavioral standards. Living the values is essential to create an environment that reinforces our dedication to our values/mission.

The importance of core values:

- Core values are part of the ideology so deeply held that they will never be compromised.
- The core ideology does not change, even in our changing environments.

- The core values of the company will withstand any change in leadership.
- Future employees are hired with similar values – they are not expected to adapt to our values.
- These values guide all behaviors, guidelines, and standards.
- We continually ask ourselves if decisions or activities are in alignment with our core values.

Our Core Values

Integrity: We pride ourselves on being impeccable with our word, fervent in our passion for this city and our craft. We only sell beer we're proud to present.

Teamwork: We are a team first. Like a great team, we help each other and hold each other accountable to live our values.

Generosity: We are driven to help. We are giving of our time, skill, and resources to aid worthwhile local causes.

Respect: We are all equals. We treat every employee and every customer like they are part of our family.

Innovation: Our beer will be thoughtfully crafted, locally unique, and made with community in mind. We take pride in creativity and trendsetting product.

Measurable Achievement: Perfect Plain Brewing Company measures outcomes using evidence-based practices, innovative technologies, surveying, and other improvement methodologies to assure return on investment for all stakeholders.

Standards of Behavior

Commitment to Coworkers

- Conduct ourselves with the idea that the result of great teamwork is success for our partners and all Perfect Plain Brewing Company team members.

- If serving on a team, hold yourself trustworthy and accountable.
- Be flexible and supportive – set an example of cooperation.
- Greet each other with a smile, verbal acknowledgment, and be helpful and compassionate to all.
- Recognize the value of each individual.
- Be respectful of your coworker's privacy.
- Respect diversity – treat each other with fairness and equality.
- Be honest in dealing with others – inside or outside the office.
- Respect each other's time by being on time for all meetings/ appointments.
- Always keep your word; others are depending on you.

Professional Conduct/Attitude

- Use appropriate language when you are speaking or sending e-mails.
- Refrain from disruptive behavior, discrimination, or any type of harassment.
- Demonstrate respect for all speakers, regardless of situation. Give the speaker the same respect you would want given to you if the roles were reversed.
- Do the right thing, even when no one is watching.

Appearance

- Dress in a professional manner in accordance within your entity at Perfect Plain Brewing Co. and for all meetings with partners, clients, customers, and guests. Your appearance communicates to them, "I respect you and myself."

Communication

- Do not send excessive e-mails. Please place only those who are directly related to the issue or those you would like a response from in the "To" line. If you would like to inform someone of the issue and do not want a response, please "cc" them. Send your response e-mails within 24 hours (except for weekends) only to the person sending the note unless it is necessary or asked for all to read your response.
- Keep personal phone calls to a minimum and never while working behind the bar in the public eye.

- When resolving issues, go directly to the coworker involved.
- Confront and manage conflict while maintaining dignity and respect for others.
- Recognize different communication styles and compromise when needed. Look for ways to communicate effectively with each other.
- Use the "5-10 Rule" anytime you come within 10 feet of a customer or coworker by making eye contact, greeting them in 5 feet with a cheerful hello, and offering assistance when necessary.

Mentoring

- Welcome, mentor, and receive new team members with energy and a "What can I do for you?" spirit.
- Teach and role model the characteristics of excellent adult learners. Specifically, when attending presentations:
  o Be totally present; engage
  o Listen as if you were going to teach it
  o Take notes write/draw/diagram
  o Relate versus compare
  o Own it

- Team members and partners horizontally and vertically. Allow others to benefit from your expertise, listen to others, and determine best practices.
- Provide assistance and resources for colleagues and partners to meet learning needs.
- Gather feedback from others, have a mentor, be a mentor, develop action plans, and follow through to push yourself and teammates to the next level.

Professional/Personal Development

- Seek self-development – utilize the tools that are provided to grow personally and professionally.
- Actively read books and other resources that are provided.
- Be a life-long learner and never stop seeking to expand skill sets.

Sense of Ownership

- Conduct ourselves as members of a "solutions" team by engaging in group problem solving. Do not just identify problems; also provide ideas for resolution.
- Do not use "We/They" when discussing issues, but phrase your communications in a neutral way that does not put others down.
- Return shared supplies or equipment to proper area.
- Keep public areas neat and clean. If the trash needs to be emptied, empty it.
- Act like an owner. Treat company resources as if they were your own – spend Perfect Plain Brewing Co. money as if it were your own and do not be frivolous or excessive.

Commitment to Partners/Clients/Customers/Guests

- Meet all promised deadlines to partners and coworkers.
- When meeting with customers, always turn your cell phone to silent and do not use the partner's, client's, customer's, or guest's time for other business.
- Keep best interests of all Perfect Plain Brewing Co. employees, peers, and those we serve in mind.
- Promote, develop, protect, improve, and preserve the reputation of the company, including all Perfect Plain Brewing Co. intellectual capital.

Commitment to Community

- Generosity is giving and giving freely; generosity is outside of what you should do; generosity is being selfless:
  o Give your time.
  o Give your praise.
  o Give your wisdom.
  o Give your support.
- Help out whenever possible – in the office or in the community. Don't wait to be asked; take initiative and volunteer. Check with your supervisor before committing to time away from work.

Managing Up

- Manage up teammates, leaders, and yourself, both externally and internally.
- Celebrate successes and have fun in our work.
- Help coworkers feel appreciated and valued – send thank you notes for specific actions.
- Do not embarrass or criticize partners, clients, customers, guests, or coworkers in the presence of others.
- Do not gossip or talk negatively about others.

COMMITMENT STATEMENT

Perfect Plain Brewing Company will be a success because of our employees. We practice what we teach and believe that through our values and standards of behavior we will create and maintain a culture that makes any of our companies a great place to work.

We have described certain values and standards of behavior that are expected from our employees in our "values-based" company. We model our behavioral guidelines and are committed to success. Our values guide the exceptional service we provide to all we serve.

You play an important role in helping us achieve our goals and fulfill our Mission: To create incredible experiences that make our beer, our brewery, and our hometown, Pensacola, unforgettable.

I believe in and am committed to living these daily throughout my employment with Perfect Plain Brewing Company.

Print Name

Signature   Date

Glossary

Ambiguity
Inexactness; being open to more than one interpretation.

BBL
Abbreviation for barrel, the unit of volume used in brewing. One beer barrel equals 31 gallons.

COGS
Cost of Goods Sold.

Billboard Distribution
The strategy of distribution that is not primarily focused on generating profit, but instead is curated, in very limited form, with the purpose of driving additional taproom sales after gaining exposure of the brand at an offsite location.

Daily Report
A report filled out by the closing leader that outlines daily sales, any specific people who came into the brewery, any issues that need to be fixed, and so on.

Distribution model
Beer sales that are made offsite from the brewery (i.e. bars, restaurants). The laws regarding beer distribution vary from state to state.

Employee Engagement

The extent in which employees engage within a company, including high morale, commitment to their job and coworkers, and overall happiness of working at a particular place.

Equity Financing

The process of building startup capital by selling off equity, or ownership, in your company.

Employee Engagement Survey

A survey conducted to measure the engagement of a company's employees. We suggest conducting one at least once per year.

Family Meetings

A weekly Monday meeting of every supervisor at Perfect Plain Brewing Company where we discuss the previous week, consider what's coming up, and synergize our efforts.

Gross Margin

The difference between the cost to produce an item – like a barrel of beer – and what the item is sold for.

Peer Interview

The third step of the three-tier interviewing process where the interviewee's peers conduct an interview with the candidate and ultimately make the decision on who is hired.

Programming

The process of coordinating and executing public events, festivals, specials, and the like in a taproom.

Rounding

The act of verbally engaging with customers and employees in a detailed way that drives interest, engagement, and satisfaction as well as ideas for company improvement. The term is derived from when doctors would "round" on patients in the hospital.

SBA

Small Business Administration, a U.S. government agency that provides support to entrepreneurs and small businesses.

Self-Distribution
Beer sold to offsite locations (bars, restaurants, etc.) directly by the manufacturer and *not* through a third-party distribution company.

Taproom Model
The brewery, distillery, or cidery model that relies on the vast majority of its sales to be generated on site at the company's taproom. The rules governing taproom sales, and what can be sold in a taproom, vary from state to state.

Top Line Revenue
The gross amount of money generated by a company for the sale of goods and services.

TTB
The Alcohol and Tobacco Tax and Trade Bureau. A bureau of the United States treasury, the TTB administers Brewer's Notices, which is the federal license that allows a brewery to operate. The TTB also collects all federal excise taxes on the production of beer.

Taproom Model
The brewery, distillery, or cidery model that relies on the vast majority of its sales to be generated on site at the company's taproom. The rules governing taproom sales, and what can be sold in a taproom, vary from state to state.

We/They
A barrier to strong culture, we/they is when an owner, manager, or employee takes the company's "wins" or "good news" as their own doing, and gives away the losses by blaming/rationalizing those on someone else, most commonly the owner, manager, or company itself.

About the Author

D.C. REEVES IS an entrepreneur and writer who has helped lead Perfect Plain Brewing Co. to become one of Florida's top microbrewery success stories.

He spent more than a decade as an award-winning journalist, covering major college football at Florida State University and University of Alabama. The newspaper life – one part fun, one part deadline-induced anxiety – led him to a newfound love while traveling for work: craft beer.

D.C.'s travels and moves around the nation as a sportswriter also meant a burgeoning taste for high-quality local beer as well as an immense appreciation for the immersive craft beer experience.

He returned to his hometown, Pensacola, Florida, in 2015 with the thirst to create his dream. In 2016 he narrowed his focus and drained his retirement account to 53 cents to start Perfect Plain.

As his two-year process to create and operate a successful microbrewery began, so did D.C.'s skill set to create an excellent organization. He serves as the chief of staff to Quint Studer, the founder of Studer Group, the most renowned healthcare consulting company in the United States.

D.C. took these lessons taught by Studer the nation's best healthcare systems, and retrofitted and realigned those practices to work in the craft beer world.

He learned about successful entrepreneurship through building a great customer experience and an awesome place to work, happiness that in each and every case cascades down to create customer satisfaction and financial success.

Despite being tucked away in the northwest tip of Florida, Perfect Plain Brewing Company became one of the busiest taprooms in the state in its first year of operations. Better yet, D.C. logged his experiences so that one day he could share those with entrepreneurs looking to start their dream brewery, cidery, or distillery. In August 2019, Perfect Plain expanded to open Garden & Grain, an immersive garden cocktail program and experience built behind the brewery in a former feed and seed warehouse on a plot of land first planned as Pensacola family gardens in 1764.

Since opening Perfect Plain, D.C. has become a mentor and consultant to breweries as well as prospective and current small business owners looking to start and grow their own great company and become an integral part of the community.

Index